Collins éHow

HOW TO DO
just about
everything
in the
OFFICE

Courtney Rosen & the eHow Editors

HarperCollins*Publishers*
Westerhill Road, Glasgow G64 2QT
www.collins.co.uk

This selection from *How To Do Just About Everything* first published by
HarperCollinsPublishers 2004

ISBN 0-00-719372-6

A catalogue record for this book is available from the British Library.

Printed and bound in Great Britain by Clays Ltd, St Ives plc
1

UK Edition Produced by Grant Laing Partnership
Editors: Jane Simmonds, Helen Ridge and Terry Burrows
Designer: Christine Lacey

eHow, Inc.
Editor-in-Chief: William R. Marken
Book Editor: Sharon Rose Beaulaurier
Editors: Dale Conour, Julie Jares,
Jason Jensen,
Roberta Kramer, Deborah McCaskey,
Jill Metzler,
Sonya Mukherjee, Mimi Towle
Editorial Assistants: Shawn Asim,
Linette Kim, Alison Goldberg,
Matt Holohan
Creative Director: Patrick Barrett

Founder: Courtney Rosen
CFO: Mark Murray
VP of Engineering: Gladys Barnes
Director of Business Development:
Jose Guerrero
General Counsel: James M. Hackett
VP of Commerce: Josh Prince
VP of Marketing: Kristen Sager
VP of Operations: Jeff Tinker
VP of Product Strategy:
Joseph A. Vause
VP of Sales: Kevin Walsh

.com press
CEO: John Owen
President: Terry Newell
COO: Larry Partington
VP, International Sales:
Stuart Laurence
VP, Publisher: Roger Shaw
Creative Director: Gaye Allen

Managing Editor: Janet Goldenberg
Art Director: Diane Dempsey
Series Manager: Brynn Breuner
Production & Layout: Joan Olson,
Lorna Strutt
Production Director:
Chris Hemesath

Project Coordinators:
Margaret Garrou, Lorna Strutt
Contributing Edictors: Mandy
Erickson, Norman Kolpas
Copy Chief: Elissa Rabellino
Copy Editors: Linda Bouchard,
Claire Breen, Kathy Kaiser, Gail
Nelson, Cynthia Rubin, David Sweet
Proofreader: Ruth Jacobson
Indexer: Ken DellaPenta

Courtney Rosen and other contributors to this book appear on behalf of
eHow, Inc.

.com|press
.com press is a division of Weldon Owen Inc., 814 Montgomery Street,
San Francisco, California 94133

BUSINESS

Running a Small Business

COMPUTERS

Computer Equipment

Computer Skills

RUNNING THE OFFICE

First Aid

OFFICE LIFE

Self-Improvement

Business Manners

A Note to Readers

When attempting any of the described activities in this book, please note the following:

Risky activities Certain activities described in this book are inherently dangerous or risky. Before attempting any new activity, make sure you are aware of your own limitations and consider all applicable risks (whether listed or not).

Professional advice While we strive to provide complete and accurate information, it is not intended as a substitute for professional advice. You should always consult a professional whenever appropriate, or if you have any questions or concerns regarding medical, legal or financial advice.

Physical or health-related activities Be sure to consult your GP before attempting any health- or diet-related activity, or any activity involving physical exertion, particularly if you have any condition that could impair or limit your ability to engage in such an activity.

Adult supervision The activities described in this book are intended for adults only, and they should not be performed by children without responsible adult supervision.

Breaking the law The information provided in this book should not be used to break any applicable law or regulation.

All of the information in this book is obtained from sources that we believe are accurate and reliable. However, we make no warranty, express or implied, that the information is sufficient or appropriate for every individual, situation or purpose. Further, the information may become out of date over time. You assume the risk and full responsibility for all your actions, and eHow, Inc. and the publishers will not be liable for any loss or damage of any sort, whether consequential, incidental, special or otherwise, that may result from the information presented. The descriptions of third-party products and services in this book are for information only and are not intended as an endorsement by eHow, Inc. of any particular product or service.

Skill-level icons – ⌐ – indicate the ease or difficulty of each undertaking on a scale of one to five, with one being the easiest. In the last few pages you'll also find a keyword index to help you locate instructions for every task quickly.

1

Take Meeting and Lecture Notes

There are many ways to take meeting notes. The "trigger" method shown here is time-tested and widely practised.

⊙ **Steps**

1 Write down the date.

2 Draw a vertical line down the lined portion of the page, about one-third of the way over from the left margin.

3 Write down categories and questions on the left side of the line as the meeting proceeds.

4 Put specifics and answers on the right side of the line.

5 Use abbreviations to keep up with your lecturer. Simple symbols include an up arrow (↑) for "increase" and a right arrow (→) for "leads to" or "results in".

6 Note anything you're unclear about at the top of the page, and ask about it during the question period.

✱ **Tips**

Number your lists for easier structuring and recall.

Review your meeting notes during the evening of the day you took them. This should help the knowledge stick in your mind.

2

Research a Subject on the Internet

If you know where to look and what sources to trust, the internet can be a great tool for conducting research.

⊙ **Steps**

1 Begin your search with a web search engine. Enter keywords or phrases related to the subject matter that interests you, and click Search.

2 In the results list, click on a site's name to go to it. Even if the site doesn't have what you're looking for, check to see if it has links to other sites that might be more useful. Use the Back button on your browser to return to the original results list.

3 If the first list had too many or too few results, tinker with your keywords to produce more focused search results.

4 Go to some of the many online encyclopedias for information about your subject. You'll find them under the Reference heading at a subject-indexed search site such as Yahoo! From the encyclopedia's search page, enter keywords and phrases related to your subject.

5 Go to sites that specialise in internet research. These sites offer links to research materials and will sometimes do your research for you.

6 Look for online library catalogues. Some provide online access to the full text of certain articles and books.

7 Check out internet newsgroups on your subject. You can even post a request for information.

8 Visit chat rooms that are related to your subject matter.

✱ Tip

Use multiple search engines to get a variety of search results: the same keywords can yield very different answers.

⚠ Warning

Always consider the source of information: university web pages and government sources tend to be more reliable than those belonging to individuals or businesses with vested interests.

Research a Subject in the Library

The library is an excellent place to begin researching a subject. Works are catalogued either in a computer database or – in older libraries – on cards in drawers.

⊙ Steps

1 Check the computer database, if your library has one. Go to a computer terminal and enter a keyword or phrase from the subject matter you wish to research. Most systems will allow you to enter a specific author, title or subject. If you are searching for newspaper, magazine or journal articles, look in an online periodical index. Note that there are indexes for specialised subject areas, such as medicine.

2 Make a note of the item's unique code: this will indicate where the book, magazine or microfilm can be found, as well as its availability status (whether or not it's on loan to another reader). At some libraries you can print or e-mail this information.

3 Alternatively, find your library's card catalogue. This is a stack of drawers containing an enormous number of note cards stored in alphabetical order. Every item in the library should have three note cards: an author card, a title card and a subject-heading card. These are often filed in separate sets of drawers. For newspaper, magazine and journal articles – especially older ones that may not be indexed in computer databases – ask a librarian to recommend the appropriate periodical index to use. Older periodical indexes are usually in book form. When you find the appropriate item, look for its code number.

4 Make a list of as many code numbers on your topic as you can find before taking them along to the bookshelves. Try rephrasing your keywords and subjects to find a broad range of books that you can narrow down after some browsing. To make life easier when searching the bookshelves, make note of the codes on your list that are close to each other.

5 Find the section in the library that corresponds to the code number of your item. Some books and periodicals may be in storage and may have to be ordered in advance.

6 Remember that librarians are paid to help library users. If you need help, ask someone.

Education and Careers

✳ Tips

When you find an item in the non-fiction stacks, it will usually be surrounded by many other works on the same subject. Browse the surrounding works for extra research material.

Most modern libraries offer not only books and periodicals but also microfilm, videos, audio resources and possibly internet connections. Ask your librarian for details.

Most libraries have photocopiers. Rather than borrow a large number of books, make copies of just the pages with the material you need. Note which books they're from.

If your library doesn't have the material you need, ask a librarian about arranging for an inter-library loan.

4

Read Quickly and Effectively

Sail through the barrage of information out there by using some key reading and skimming skills.

◉ Steps

1   Read different materials at different speeds: skim or speed-read less important items, and save critical or difficult works for when you are most alert and have time.

2   Pick out the main ideas of a book by reading its cover flaps or scanning the table of contents. Use the index to locate key words quickly.

3   Survey the layout of your reading material. Look at the title and section headings and piece together its logical flow. This framework will guide you in reading the piece more carefully.

4   If you need to skim, try reading the first sentence of each paragraph (which is usually a topic sentence) to get a general idea of its content.

5   Practise reading more quickly by moving your index finger down a row of text at a speed slightly faster than your normal reading speed.

Learning Skills

6   Underline sparingly so the truly useful information doesn't get lost.

7   Jot down quick notes, questions or thoughts that will make it easier to refer to the material later. Taking notes also makes for active reading and better retention of important points.

*Tips

Increasing your vocabulary will help you to improve your reading speed.

Take a speed-reading course – there are many available.

5

Take Reading Notes

Remembering what you read will help your work, and taking good reading notes will help you retain what you've read.

⊙ Steps

1   Budget enough time for taking notes. The time you spend now will pay off with less review time and increased retention.

2   Date your notes, and write full bibliographic information next to the date, including author, title, publication, date of publication, city, publisher, and volume number for journal articles.

3   Take notes in outline form to structure the material, and break it into related sections and sub-sections.

4   Use the structure of the book (or article) as the structure of your notes. For instance, chapters correspond to major headings, chapter sections to sub-headings.

5   Note anything that is pertinent to the author's argument; try to avoid trivial minutiae. Important points tend to be contained in introductory and concluding paragraphs.

6   Distinguish facts from opinions, and quotations from summaries, in a way that will make it clear which is which when you review your notes.

7   Review your reading notes the next day, and do it again a few days later. This is a time-efficient way of retaining the material.

✻ Tips

Consider using index cards if you're taking notes for a research paper. Be sure that you list the bibliographic information on a separate, numbered card.

One way of deciding what is relevant is to "cheat" by reading the conclusion first so that you'll know what's important as soon as you come across it in the text.

Use abbreviations in your notes: for instance, an up arrow (↑) for "increase" and a delta (Δ) for "change".

6

Outline a Paper

An outline helps you organise a paper's content in a logical and sequential way. Here is a basic guide.

⊙ Steps

1   Write your composition's working title at the top of a blank sheet of paper. It does not need to be the one you use for your final paper.

2   Beneath the working title, write a few lines about the purpose of the paper and the steps you will take to achieve that goal. For example: "In this paper, I will show the secrets of a successful and happy life, using scholarly journals from psychologists and vets."

3   Follow the summary with a statement of your paper's thesis: for example, "Owning a dog can make one's life healthier and happier".

4   Begin to lay down the basic framework for your paper by dividing its content into sections.

5   Start by writing either an Arabic (1) or Roman (I) numeral one – depending on your style of outline – followed by a full stop, then the title of the section (a "section heading"). In an informal outline use Arabic numerals; in a formal outline use Roman numerals.

6   Follow this with a few lines describing what you wish to accomplish in the section.

Learning Skills

7   Use sub-sections to list specific examples or topics that you wish to discuss under each heading. Mark them with a lowercase letter (*a*, *b*, *c* and so on).

8   Follow this format for each section heading, then put the sections in the following general order: introduction, body, conclusion.

✳ Tips

You may find it helpful to write each section heading on a separate sheet of paper to allow yourself room to take notes and brainstorm.

Remember that the outline is merely a tool in the writing process – it does not bind you to anything. Feel free to change its format to suit your needs.

As you write your paper, refer back to your outline to make sure you're on track.

7

Write a Paper

Writing a good research paper can be a tough challenge, but breaking it down into smaller pieces helps a lot.

◎ Steps

1   Choose a topic that is broad enough to be interesting but narrow enough to be manageable.

2   Find your sources. Start with three or four, check their bibliographies for additional sources, and repeat the process until you have sufficient material with which to work.

3   Reserve one index card for each of your sources. Record the bibliographic information for the source on its index card, and number each card for ease of future reference.

4   Take reading notes on index cards, writing down only the material that is most relevant to your project. Write the source number on each card.

5   Organise your index cards by topic and sub-topic.

6   Use the cards as a basis for an outline.

Education and Careers

7 Write an introduction that grabs the reader and plots out the trajectory of your argument.

8 Write the body of the paper, following the structure you created in your outline. Be sure to cite sources.

9 Write the conclusion, reviewing how you've made your points.

10 Come up with a title after you've written the paper, not before: you don't want the content of the paper to be hamstrung by an inappropriate title.

11 Read your paper at least twice to be sure your argument makes sense and is presented logically.

12 Proofread carefully; academics hate typographical errors. Use your word processor's spell checker, but don't rely on it wholly.

Tips

Avoid letting the size of a project daunt you. Stay focused on each task, and remember that if you do those well, you'll end up with an excellent research paper.

Use bibliography software to help manage your sources. Consult a style guide for details on citation of sources.

Consider taking a class on writing research papers.

Don't leave such a difficult task to the last minute. Start early, and work gradually.

⚠ Warning

Be sure to cite your sources whenever you make use of an idea from someone else.

Improve Your Memory

Scores of books, videos, web sites and seminars are devoted to memory enhancement. The steps below summarise the main points of most techniques.

⊙ Steps

1 Make sure you're alert and attentive before trying to memorise anything.

2 Understand the material rather than merely memorising it, if it's the type that requires deeper comprehension.

3 Look for larger patterns or ideas, and organise pieces of information into meaningful groups.

4 Link newly acquired knowledge with what you already know. Place what you learn into context with the rest of your knowledge, looking out for relationships between ideas.

5 Engage your visual and auditory senses by using drawings, charts or music to aid memory. Creating a memorable mental picture can also help.

6 Use mnemonics – devices such as formulas or rhymes that serve as memory aids. For example, use the acronym "HOMES" to memorise America's Great Lakes (Huron, Ontario, Michigan, Erie and Superior).

7 Repeat and review what you've learned as many times as you can. Apply it or use it in conversation, as continual practice is the key to remembering things in the long term.

✱ Tips

Review the things you have memorised right before going to sleep; this might help you recall it better in the morning.

Things that interest you are easier to remember. Try to develop an interest in what you're memorising.

Your memory and thinking will function much better if you're in good health, well-rested and properly hydrated.

Try writing down or reciting aloud what you've memorised – this can help etch it in your mind.

Education and Careers

Cram for an Exam

While not an ideal style of study, cramming is an inevitable part of student life. Focus on general concepts, memory techniques and relaxation.

⊙ Steps

1 Compose yourself. Relax and take several deep breaths to clear your mind of clutter and stress.

2 Cover the most difficult information first.

3 Review the main points, general ideas and broad, sweeping concepts. These are essential to understanding the more detailed points on which you will be tested.

4 Skim lecture notes and assigned reading materials (see 4 "Read Quickly and Effectively").

5 Take breaks to stretch, relax, eat or exercise. As a general rule, you should take a break for 10 minutes out of every hour.

6 Review the main points and concepts one more time and then get some sleep before the big exam.

✳ Tips

Go easy on the caffeine and sugar. The initial boost from these substances will inevitably be followed by a crash.

Nourish yourself. Eat a good meal with a balanced ratio of carbohydrates to proteins. Avoid overeating, which tends to cause sluggishness.

⚠ Warning

Avoid staying up all night before an exam. Depriving yourself of sleep may hurt more than it helps.

Learning Skills

Break the Procrastination Habit

There's an old joke that the members of Procrastinators Anonymous plan to meet ... but keep putting it off.

◎ Steps

1 Think about why you procrastinate: Are you afraid of failing at the task? Are you a perfectionist and only willing to begin working after every little element is in place? Are you easily distracted?

2 Break up a large, difficult project into several smaller pieces.

3 Set deadlines for completion. Try assigning yourself small-scale deadlines: for example, commit to reading a certain number of pages in the next hour.

4 Work in small blocks of time instead of in long stretches. Try studying in one- to two-hour spurts, allowing yourself a small break after each stint.

5 Start with the easiest aspect of a large, complex project. For example, if you're writing an academic paper and find that the introduction is turning out to be difficult to write, start with the paper's body instead.

6 Enlist others to help. Make a bet with your family, friends or co-workers that you will finish a particular project by a specified time, or find other ways to make yourself accountable.

7 Eliminate distractions or move to a place where you can concentrate. Turn off the television, the phone ringer, the radio and anything else that might keep you from your task.

✱ Tip

Remember that progress, not perfection, is your goal.

Education and Careers

Find Out Your IQ

Though IQ (intelligence quotient) has come under scrutiny as a measure of intelligence, finding out your IQ can help you join certain organisations and can open other doors for you.

◎ Steps

1 Find an appropriate IQ test – there are a great many out there. On the web, consider visiting iqtest.com to take an IQ test and to get general information about the process.

2 Take the test and score it.

3 Take several more tests and average the scores, dropping the lowest and highest. The result will give a good approximation of your IQ.

4 Understand the results. Generally, an IQ of 100 places you in the 50th percentile (exactly average); 110 puts you in the 75th percentile; 120 in the 93rd; and 130 in the 98th, which is high enough to join Mensa.

5 Remember that no single number can measure something as complex as intelligence. Instead, IQ is intended to measure your chances of academic success in schools.

✱ Tip

Be aware that high-IQ societies such as Mensa usually accept the results of only certain IQ tests. Contact individual societies to find out their requirements (see 12 "Join Mensa").

⚠ Warning

Bear in mind that there are many important human "intelligences" that standard IQ tests can't measure, such as musical or artistic talent, social ability, physical coordination, ambition and sense of humour.

Join Mensa

Mensa is an international organisation of people in the top two per cent of the intelligence range. Founded in England in 1946, it now has more than 100,000 members. Here's how to join.

⊙ Steps

1 Bear in mind that testing in the top two per cent on an accepted IQ test or standardised test is the only membership criterion.

2 Visit the Mensa website (mensa.org.uk) to get the information you'll need to complete the steps below. Alternatively, call (01902) 772771 or send a letter to British Mensa Limited, St John's House, St John's Square, Wolverhampton, WV2 4AH.

3 Find out if Mensa will accept the results of an intelligence test you've already taken. Mensa also accepts scores from approximately 200 standardised tests (such as the LSAT or GMAT).

4 Order official test results from the appropriate testing company and send them to Mensa.

5 Contact your nearest Mensa office to take the official Mensa test, if you haven't qualified through another test.

6 Be prepared to pay annual fees if you're admitted.

✳ Tips

Visit Mensa's website to get more detailed information for your specific situation.

As a Mensa member, you'll be able to interact with other Mensa members at social events, through publications and during various activities.

Get a Job

Good timing plays a role in finding a job, but that's only part of the picture. Here's how to find the job you want.

⊙Steps

1. Assess your skills, experience and goals, and look into appropriate employment fields that interest you.

2. Spread the word. Tell everyone you know and meet that you are looking for a job – you will be surprised at the number of opportunities you may discover this way.

3. Network, network, network. Attend professional-association meetings in your industry, scour the associations' membership directories for contacts, and schedule informational interviews with people in the field. Always try to get more names of people to contact at the end of the informational interview. Volunteer for something.

4. For resources and leads, contact your local employment office or your school/university careers advisor.

5. Get out and about. The most direct way to learn about job openings is to contact employers themselves. Target an area, dress the part, and stop in at every appropriate business establishment, including employment agencies, to fill out an application.

6. Remember that many job openings are not listed in the newspaper job section. However, internet job boards are often used by employers for their ease and immediacy.

7. Pick up the telephone. It may be scary – and you will hear "No" a lot – but you may only need to hear "Yes" a few times to land a job.

8. Follow up on written contacts. Send out CVs and fill out applications, but understand that these alone won't land you a job. Follow up with a phone call within five to seven days of every written communication.

9. Ask for interviews. If you find yourself being interviewed for a position that's not right for you (or with an interviewer who doesn't think you're right for the opening), request interviews with other department heads for resources and leads, or even with other companies that the interviewer may know are recruiting.

Job Search

10 Prepare. Do some research on the hiring company and its industry so that you'll have a stock of relevant questions to ask the person across the desk.

11 Give the impression that you're ready to be part of the team.

12 Send a thank-you note after the interview. E-mail is acceptable.

13 Call your interviewer three days later and ask if there is any further information you can provide.

✳ Tips

When you're being interviewed, make it a dialogue. Asking questions will make you appear knowledgeable and eager, as well as help to calm your nerves.

Review the Sunday job section to get a feel for the hiring marketplace.

Drop in on your local chamber of commerce breakfast or after-dinner meeting. These are usually open to non-members for a small fee and offer the opportunity to make valuable contacts.

See 17 "Speed Up a Job Hunt" for additional pointers.

⚠ Warning

Avoid making the mistake of turning down additional interviews once you've had a good one. Keep your job search in high gear right up until your first day on the new job.

14

Find a Job Online

The internet is rewriting the rules of the job-search game. Make sure that you know all the ways to find a job online.

◎ Steps

1 Peruse the websites of any companies that may interest you. Most companies will post job openings on their sites.

2 Go to a website specifically geared towards finding jobs. You can search for jobs on these sites by career field, location and even potential salary.

3   If you're a student, your school or university may have a careers advice web page with job listings, guidance for writing CVs and advice on being interviewed.

4   Visit an online newspaper and search the classifieds section for job adverts and job opportunities. Many newspapers – national and local – have web pages.

5   Check out search engines, as these also feature classified sections. Browse according to your location and interests.

*Tips

Search frequently: new job listings are posted every day.

Many sites offer services that will allow you to e-mail your cv directly to a potential employer.

⚠ Warning

Some sites designed specifically for finding jobs may require a membership fee. Read the small print before signing up.

15
Network Effectively

Networking can help you to get a job or otherwise expand your business horizons. The key to successful networking is taking the initiative – and refining your conversational skills.

⊙ Steps

1   Talk to people you don't know, everywhere you go. Cocktail parties and weddings are just the tip of the iceberg; don't forget about aeroplanes, supermarket queues, sports events, festivals, bookshops and so on.

2   Learn to ask "What do you do?" with comfort, sincerity and interest.

3   Become a better listener. Ask a question and then be quiet until you hear the answer.

4   Practise the way you present your own skills. Learn more than one approach, whether frank or subtle.

5   Keep a great updated brochure, business card or some other form of information about yourself on you at all times. Get comfortable with handing out your card.

6   Take classes to improve your public speaking, body language and writing skills.

7   Join every networking club and association in your field.

8   Follow up on any lead, no matter how minor.

✱ Tips

Make news so that you can get your name out there. Be the dog walker who gets on the evening news for organising the Doggy Olympics.

Stay in touch with people you like and respect even if they can't help you immediately. You don't want to go to someone only when you are desperate.

16

Prepare a Basic CV

There are as many kinds of CV as there are jobs. Use a style that matches your personality and career objectives.

◉ Steps

1   Choose one or two fonts at most, and avoid underlined, boldfaced and italic text. Some companies use automated recruiting systems that have difficulty with special formatting.

2   Opt for the active voice rather than the passive voice (say "met the goal" rather than "the goal was met").

3   Provide contact information such as your home address, telephone number and e-mail address at the top of your CV.

4   Include an objectives statement, in which you use clear, simple language to indicate what kind of job you're looking for. This should appear below your contact information.

5   List your most recent and relevant experience first. Include time
    frames, company names and job titles, followed by major
    responsibilities.

6   In a second section, outline your education, awards, accomplishments
    and anything else you wish prospective employers to know about you.

7   Hire a proofreader or ask someone you trust to proofread your CV.
    Mistakes in spelling, grammar or syntax can land it in the bin.

8   Limit your CV to one page unless it is scientific or highly technical.
    Less is definitely more when it comes to CVs.

9   Write a cover letter to submit with your CV (see 19 "Write an Effective
    Covering Letter").

Tips

Refrain from using "I" in your CV.

Leave out personal information, particularly as it relates to your age,
race, religious background and sexual orientation.

Avoid obscure fonts, clip art and other unnecessary visuals.

✓ 17 Speed Up a Job Hunt

When you're looking for a job, it's all too easy to let yourself be lulled by the familiar rhythms of home or work life. Before you know it, another month has gone by and you're still out of work or unhappily employed. Here are some ways to jump-start your job search and get your career in gear.

Know yourself

☐ Make a list of your skills. Note which ones you're most interested in using, and which are most likely to interest employers.

☐ Identify the skills that you haven't had the chance to use in your current or most recent job. Which ones are of greatest importance to you?

☐ Think about how you can use your favourite skills in a new job. Set specific short-term and long-term goals to guide your job search.

☐ Decide which of your short-term goals are negotiable and which are not.

☐ Write a two-minute speech describing your experience, skills and goals. Rehearse it.

Brush up job-seeking skills

☐ Hire a proofreader to catch any errors in your CV.

☐ Ask a friend or colleague to grill you about your experience so you can practise your answers.

☐ Videotape yourself in a mock interview to see how you come across.

☐ Hire a consultant to look at your CV and teach you some interview techniques.

☐ Make sure you have clean, wrinkle-free professional attire ready to wear for job interviews.

Get organised

☐ Make a list of leads: people you know, people they've referred you to and companies that interest you.

☐ Set goals – for example, to send out ten CVs this week, make five cold calls or conduct two informational interviews.

☐ Make weekly and daily to-do lists, and check off each item as it's completed.

☐ Keep files or notebooks with details of everyone you've written to, called or who has interviewed you, and anything you want to remember. Include job listings and contacts' business cards.

☐ Keep your filing system handy and well-organised so you can refer to it quickly in case of a phone call.

Research and target employers

☐ Read trade publications to learn about companies in your field and determine which ones may be hiring.

☐ Talk to friends or acquaintances in the field for the inside scoop on companies.

☐ Set up informational interviews or ask to spend a day with someone who has the type of job you're seeking.

☐ Aim your cover letters to individuals who may be in a position to hire you – send a copy to the personnel department as well.

☐ After scheduling an interview, search the web for more facts about the company.

☐ Ask the company for a press kit or annual report if it's not available on the web.

☐ Make a list of questions that show your knowledge and interest in the company.

Job Search

Write a CV When Changing Careers

Your CV should change along with your career goals. Here are some ways to restructure and polish your CV as you move towards a new profession or career.

⊙ Steps

1 Read up on the skills and requirements for the new career or job you are seeking. Look at job listings in the newspaper or online to get an idea of what skills you'll need to break in.

2 Make a list of the skills and requirements you discovered in step 1. Your new CV will need to focus on them.

3 Compare the skills and requirements on that list with those listed on your current CV, underlining the qualifications both have in common. These are the skills that will carry over to your new CV.

4 Rewrite the CV to highlight the skills that apply to your new career. Focus on your strengths, experience and education in these areas.

5 Change the focus of your CV. If you are a pharmacologist trying to break into pharmaceutical sales, for example, focus on your experience with different vendors and other tasks that relate to sales.

6 Think of any other experiences relevant to the skills on your list – this may include volunteer work, work experience, hobbies and travel. Work all of these experiences into your CV.

✳ Tips

Consider volunteering, work experience or taking a second job within your new area of interest to gain practical experience.

If you don't feel you can write an effective CV, specialised services can do it for you. Look on the internet under "CV service".

⚠ Warning

You may have to settle for a lower-paid job until you can build up your experience – and hence your CV – when changing careers.

Write an Effective Covering Letter

A CV is an essential tool for any job search, but it's not the only tool. Your covering letter is equally important.

⊙ Steps

1 Find a job posting, job tip or advertisement that interests you, and make sure you are truly qualified for the position. Busy employers sometimes receive hundreds of letters, so don't waste their time or yours.

2 Match the letterhead style and paper you will use for your cover letter to that of your CV. This helps to establish a solid first impression.

3 Don't bother with the salutation if you do not know the name of the person who will be reviewing your CV. It's best to address the letter to a specific person; call the company and see if the receptionist can give you a name and title.

4 Grab the reader's attention right away – make him or her want to keep reading. You need to distinguish yourself early from the rest of the pack.

5 Mention in the first paragraph where you learned about this particular job opportunity and why you're interested.

6 Establish a professional image in the second and third paragraphs by highlighting your most significant accomplishments and qualifications. Be careful not to quote your CV verbatim.

7 Clarify what you can contribute to the employer's organisation rather than what you hope to gain from this potential relationship. You can discuss the latter in the interview.

8 In the last paragraph, remind the reader that your CV will explain your qualifications, experience and education. Request a personal interview, and indicate the times you will be available.

9 Close your letter by telling the reader that you look forward to hearing from the company, and restate your enthusiasm for learning more about the opportunity.

10 Double-check your document for spelling and grammar; refer to a stylebook if necessary. Carelessness makes a bad impression on employers.

11 Print your letter using a good ink-jet or laser printer.

✳ Tips

Before writing your covering letter, research the company to which you're applying. Then your letter can refer to specifics about the employer's business as reasons for your interest in working there.

Keep it short. Most covering letters are one page and use a standard business-letter format (see 28 "Write a Formal Business Letter").

Consider using bullet points in your middle paragraphs to further highlight accomplishments.

Avoid getting too personal or wordy. Save stories and relevant anecdotes for the interview.

Avoid bragging. Confidence is important, but don't overdo it.

⚠ Warning

Never send a photocopied letter or use a form letter. This tells the prospective employer that you are not interested enough to write an original letter.

20

Succeed at a Job Interview

Most interviewers form their opinion of you in the first few minutes of a meeting. Here's how to make a good impression.

◎ Steps

1 In the days before your interview, talk to people who have worked at the company. If it's practical, hang around outside the building while employees are arriving and note how they dress and behave.

2 Learn the name and title of the person you'll be meeting. Arrive at least ten minutes early to collect your thoughts.

3   Take time to greet and acknowledge the secretary or administrative
    assistant; it's good old-fashioned courtesy, and besides, this person
    may have a lot of influence.

4   Bring along an extra copy of your CV or letters of recommendation in
    case the interviewer doesn't have them handy.

5   Be open and upbeat. Face your interviewer with arms and legs
    uncrossed, head up, and hands and face at ease. Smile and look the
    interviewer in the eye.

6   Know the company's business, target clients, market and direction.

7   Walk in prepared with a few relevant questions and listen carefully.

8   Subtly give the impression that you're already part of the team by
    using "we" when asking how something is done. For example, say,
    "How do we deal with the press?"

9   Conclude with a positive statement and a quick, firm handshake. Ask
    when you might follow up, and get a business card from the
    interviewer.

10 Send a thank-you note.

✳ Tip

Avoid asking about money at the start of the interview.

21

Request a Reference From a Former Employer

**A good employment reference can seal that job offer that
you've worked hard to win.**

◎ Steps

1   Get references before you need them. Managers make job changes,
    too, and time can erase the memory of even the most outstanding
    employee.

2   Offer to write the reference letter for your former employer to review
    and sign. This saves him or her valuable time, and it allows you to

highlight the accomplishments you consider most valuable to future employers.

3 Contact former employers and other referees before offering their names to potential employers. Beyond simple courtesy, this gives you the chance to supply these people with important information such as who might be calling, the type of job you're applying for, and which of your skills you would like your referee to emphasise.

4 Acknowledge a referee with a thank-you note, even if you didn't get the job. If you did, offer a celebratory lunch.

✳ Tips

If you encounter an unhelpful policy, such as one that restricts managers from giving reference information beyond confirming job title and relevant dates of employment, ask the manager if he or she will give you a personal (rather than professional) reference.

Consider colleagues with whom you've interacted – they can be good referees, too.

22

Negotiate an Employment Contract

Be confident and careful when negotiating a new contract.

⊙ Steps

1 Research your market value before your first interview: Talk to friends and acquaintances in the business, contact headhunters, and consult career web pages that include information such as salary ranges and benefits packages.

2 Assess the company's approach, noting whether it invites negotiations or makes an offer first.

3 Listen to the way an offer is presented. A negotiation-minded manager will ask what figure you had in mind to get the process moving.

4 Delineate the different aspects of the job offer: money, benefits, stock options, responsibilities, schedules.

5 If the offer appears set, be creative in negotiating for alternative perks such as time off, relocation expenses or a travel allowance.

6   Repeat the offer out loud after you hear it, then don't say anything
    until the employer does. Your silence may be misinterpreted as
    hesitation and the employer will sweeten the pot.

7   Speak your mind if you have any concerns.

✱ Tips

Clearly demonstrate your sincere excitement and interest in the job as
well as in the compensation.

Focus on being an ally – not an adversary – throughout the negotiations.
This will keep things amiable and show that you are a team player.

23

Choose Childcare When Returning to Work

Choosing childcare can be one of the hardest decisions a new
mother (and father) have to make. There is an increasing
range available, so it is vital to make time to look at all the
options.

⊙ Steps

1   If you think you'd like to return to work after having your child, start to
    plan childcare while you are pregnant. In some areas you need to
    book a place for your child well in advance. Also, it can take
    considerable time to look at all the childcare in your area and assess
    your feelings about it.

2   Put your child first. You need to balance their needs with your family
    circumstances and your own needs as a mother or father (economic
    and emotional). Think laterally to try to find the best solution for all of
    you.

3   Investigate local childminders, daycare nurseries, nannies and au
    pairs. If you have a relative who is willing to look after your child, this
    can be a great option, but it needs to be assessed alongside others.

4   Childminders look after children in their own home. They are registered
    and inspected by Ofsted and strict rules govern how many children of

different ages they can look after. Childminders offer flexible childcare in a home environment and can become an extension of the family for many years as children grow up. Find out about them from your local authority.

5   Nurseries offer a range of options and hours. They give a sociable environment with other children and are reliably available. There are state, voluntary and private nurseries, which charge a variety of fees, all inspected by Ofsted. Find out about them from your local authority.

6   Nannies usually look after children in the child's home. They can often fit around the parents' working hours. You are responsible for their wage or salary as well as income tax and National Insurance. Find out about nannies from a nanny agency. Au pairs and mother's helps are also available.

7   Whatever childcare you look at, ask as many questions as you can think of, including: "How long have you been working with children? What is your training and qualifications? Where will my child rest? What kind of food and drink is available? What will my child do all day?"

8   When visiting childcare, look to see if the children are calm, safe and happy. Do they play together? Do the staff listen to children and answer them carefully? Do they join in with what the children are doing? Are the premises clean, safe and well-kept? Is there access outside for play?

✳ Tips

Listen to your feelings. If you are not 100 per cent happy with the childcare, don't go for it.

Talk to local parents about their experiences but remember that the final decision is yours.

Once your child is in childcare, keep an open mind and listen to him or her. Children and their needs change, childminders and nannies leave or alter their arrangements and you may have to rearrange childcare several times between babyhood and school age.

Always take up references.

⚠ Warnings

Unless a relative or highly trusted friend is looking after your child, always choose a registered childminder.

Education and Careers

Nannies who work for no more than two families at once are not registered and inspected. Unless you know a nanny personally or one is recommended by another family whom you know and trust, go through an agency when employing a nanny.

Au pairs are not usually trained to look after young children and should never be given sole responsibility for a child under three years old.

24

Help Your Child Adapt to Your Returning to Work

Not having you around all day every day is a big change for a little one. Do all you can to ease the transition.

◉ Steps

1   Give your child time to adapt. He will almost certainly protest if he is suddenly left with someone new. Spend time with your child and their new carer before leaving your child alone with the carer. Then leave the child and carer together for progressively longer. If the childcare is in a new place – the carer's home or a nursery – your child may take longer to get used to it.

2   Be calm, confident and positive at all times. These attitudes communicate themselves to your child and may help to calm him.

3   Take important toys or blankets along to the carer to ensure some continuity. Explain your child's routines, sleep times and mealtimes carefully so that the carer can keep to them as much as possible.

4   Avoid obviously temporary arrangements. If your child is happy with an arrangement, think twice about changing it. If you do need to change childcare, go through the whole process again – do not assume that your child will automatically adapt to new surroundings and people.

✱ Tips

Give yourself time to adapt, too. Initial separation from your child can be hard to deal with; ensure the carer is happy to provide progress reports and will phone you if there are any problems.

Put your child first. If he seems happy and thriving with the carer, that's the main thing. Even if a nanny or au pair doesn't do all you would wish in the way of housework stick with him or her if your child is happy.

25

Work Efficiently

We'll keep this short so you can get back to work.

⊙ Steps

1 Keep your desk and your files organised to avoid wasting time shuffling through piles of paper.

2 Go through your inbox at the beginning of each workday. Either throw away, file or follow up on each item.

3 Prioritise a list of the tasks you need to accomplish that day.

4 Delegate tasks to co-workers and assistants if possible.

5 Finish one task before you go on to the next.

6 Reduce paperwork by storing important information on your computer or electronic organiser.

7 Communicate effectively and plan carefully to make sure a job is done properly the first time around.

8 Schedule time when you'll be available and let colleagues know, to avoid constant interruptions. Close the door if you need to.

9 Take breaks. A short walk or quick lunch away from the office will increase your overall productivity.

10 Before leaving for the day, tidy up your desk and make a short list of projects you will need to do the next day.

11 Try not to take work home. You need the break.

✳ Tips

Recognise when you have the most energy in a day and do the important or harder tasks then.

Education and Careers

Note that certain days – usually Monday or Friday – are more hectic, and schedule accordingly.

Have someone else answer your telephone if possible. Give instructions about calls you wish to take and those that can be returned later.

⚠ Warnings

Avoid regularly going out for long business lunches – heavy meals make for unproductive afternoons.

Avoid procrastination (see 10 "Break the Procrastination Habit").

26

Make a To-Do List

Invest just a little time planning your day, and accomplish more things smoothly.

⊙ Steps

1 Set aside 10 to 15 minutes before you go to bed or as soon as you wake up in the morning to jot down a to-do list for the day.

2 Use any format that is comfortable for you – try writing in your daily planner. Make sure your list is on one page and can be carried with you wherever you go.

3 Try assigning tasks to hourly time slots, even if exact timing isn't crucial.

4 Fill in preset, mandatory appointments such as business meetings or child-pickup times.

5 Prioritise tasks in order of urgency, and write those down before less important ones.

6 Work out when, during the day, you are most productive and alert. Schedule the more demanding tasks during these times.

7 Schedule an easy job after a difficult one or a long task after a short one to keep yourself stimulated.

8 Indicate time for breaks and time to spend with family and friends.

9   In addition to your daily schedule, keep an ongoing list of projects that you need to accomplish but haven't pencilled into your daily list – projects to complete, bills to post, people to call. Update this list at least once a week.

10   Keep a list of long-term goals. For example, you might be planning to remodel your home or return to school for an advanced degree.

11   Make a running list for leisure or entertainment goals – books to read, films to rent, restaurants/bars/clubs to try. Write down names as you hear or read about them.

✳ Tips

Schedule things comfortably, allowing time for unexpected delays or mishaps; avoid an impossibly tight timetable.

Be sure to list everything you need to accomplish – the more you can account for, the more smoothly your day will run and the less you need to remember.

Break down large projects into specific tasks before writing them down on your list.

Feel free to revise your list as necessary, as the day goes on.

27

Delegate Responsibility

Many people delegate less than they should. Divide your assignments and hand out tasks for others to do – this will increase your overall productivity and efficiency.

⊙ Steps

1   Decide whether you want to delegate.

2   Decide to whom you want to delegate responsibility. Does this person have the necessary skills and background knowledge? How quickly will your helper learn?

3   Brief the person on the task: Define exactly what he is responsible for. Explain how the task fits into the larger project. Clarify objectives and decide on deadlines.

4 Encourage your helper to act independently and to make his own decisions by emphasising the results. Say, "I want to see such-and-such. Don't tell me the details."

5 Allow the person to perform the task. Offer help as needed, but don't be intrusive – if he has a different way of doing things than you, be flexible and open-minded about it.

6 Periodically check the standard of work. Provide helpful feedback.

7 Recognise the person who does the job – give him credit for it. Public recognition for a job well done will encourage effort in the future.

✳ Tips

Delegate tasks at times when productivity is likely to be high – try earlier in the week as opposed to Friday.

Be available to answer questions and discuss progress.

Be generous with praise for jobs that are well-executed.

⚠ Warnings

Avoid thinking that it is too much trouble to delegate responsibility – delegating will pay off over time, especially if the task needs to be done again and again.

Delegating a task doesn't mean you are no longer responsible for seeing that it's completed.

28

Write a Formal Business Letter

The business-letter format is very important for communicating formally with a company. These steps describe the "full block" format, in which all lines start at the left.

◉ Steps

1 Type the letter using word-processing software. Formal letters should not be written by hand.

2 Use your own letterhead. If you don't have a letterhead, use formal A4 stationery with a matching envelope. Avoid shop-bought note cards.

3 If you don't have a preprinted letterhead, type your name, title and return address four to six lines down from the top of the page.

4 Type the date two to six lines down from the letterhead or return address. Three lines below is the standard.

5 Choose your alignment: left aligned or justified on both sides.

6 Skip two lines and type the recipient's full name, business title and address, aligned at the left margin. Precede the name with Mr, Mrs, Ms or Dr, as appropriate.

7 Skip two to four lines and follow with your greeting, again using the formal name – "Dear Mr Jones" for example.

8 Skip two more lines and begin your letter. Introduce yourself in the first paragraph, if the recipient does not already know you. Examples: "We recently met at a seminar at the Royal Academy of Music" or "I recently purchased an insurance plan from your company".

9 Continue with the body of the letter, stating your main purpose for writing. This may be to lodge a complaint, compliment the business on its products or services, or request information. Be as concise as possible.

10 Skip two lines and conclude the letter with "Yours sincerely", followed by a comma.

11 Leave at least four blank lines for your signature, then type your name and title. Sign the letter in ink in the space created.

✳ Tips

Some people prefer to centre the date and closing section instead of aligning them at the left.

Try to keep the letter to one page. Generally, a short letter will get a quicker response than a long, rambling composition that takes several pages to come to the point.

Make certain your punctuation, spelling and grammar are letter-perfect. Use your computer's spell-check program and proofread the letter before you send it.

Education and Careers

⚠ Warning

No matter how upset you are with the recipient, try not to show your anger in your letter. You are much more likely to get the response you desire if you remain courteous.

29

Write a Speech

Composing a speech shares many of the most important aspects of preparing a paper.

◎ Steps

1 Assess how much time your speech should take. If you don't have a time limit, try to keep your speech brief yet informative.

2 Think about your audience and let your perception of the audience shape the tone of your speech as you write it.

3 Begin with an introduction establishing who you are, what your purpose is, what you'll be talking about and how long you're going to take. You may want to include a joke, anecdote or interesting fact to grab the audience's attention.

4 Organise your information into three to seven main points and prioritise them according to importance and effectiveness.

5 Delete points that aren't crucial to your speech if you have too many for your time frame.

6 Start with your most important point, then go to your least important point and move slowly back towards the most important. For example, if you have five points, with the fifth being the most important and the first being the least important, your presentation order should be 5, 1, 2, 3, 4.

7 Add support to each point using statistics, facts, examples, anecdotes, quotations or other supporting material.

8 Link your introduction, points and conclusions with smooth transitions.

9   Write a conclusion that summarises each of your points, restates your main purpose and leaves the audience with a lasting impression.

✳ Tips

The introduction should make up between 10 and 15 per cent of the total speech. The conclusion should make up 5 to 10 per cent.

When preparing your speech, make your notes easy to read by writing or printing them in large, clear letters.

Rehearse and time your speech before delivering it. Prune it if necessary.

If you are presenting a great deal of information, consider using handouts or visual aids to help your audience remember your most important points.

30

Deliver a Speech

Mastering your tone and body language is the formula for a successful delivery.

◎ Steps

1   Approach the podium confidently and put your notes in a place where you can see them easily.

2   Stand up straight with your feet shoulder-width apart. Look at your audience, pause and begin speaking. If there is no microphone, project from your diaphragm, not your throat.

3   Set the tone in your introduction with appropriate facial expressions and diction, and a specific mood.

4   Make eye contact with people in different parts of the audience, including the back row.

5   Pause briefly after you state key points to allow the audience time to absorb the information. Also, use natural and relaxed hand gestures and facial expressions to emphasise certain points.

6   Pronounce your words clearly and vary your rate, pitch and volume to keep the delivery lively.

7 Refresh your memory by periodically glancing at your notes, but avoid reading from your notes directly unless you are reading a long quotation.

8 Close your speech by thanking the audience and then confidently leaving the stage.

✳ Tips

Success come with practice. Video yourself watching out for distracting habits such saying "er" and "um" too often, or making nervous gestures.

During your speech, if you stumble on a word, it's a sign you should slow down.

31

Lead Effective Business Meetings

Too many business meetings are ill-directed, digressive and drawn out. Call a meeting only when it's absolutely critical, and structure it firmly so that it achieves its purpose.

◎ Steps

1 Decide whether you really need to call a meeting. Can the issue be resolved by an individual or a conference call?

2 Determine who needs to attend. Try keeping the number of attendees small, as large meetings get unwieldy. Suggest that people attend only the parts of the meeting that involve them. This way you can keep the discussion more focused.

3 Set definite starting and stopping times.

4 Prepare an agenda. Explain the goal of the meeting; if there are many goals, decide which ones command priority and make this clear.

5 Circulate the agenda in advance to allow attendees to prepare.

6 Assemble visual aids, such as charts, handouts or slides.

7 Start the meeting at the designated time, regardless of whether everyone is present. Avoid taking too much time to summarise for latecomers.

8. Start off the meeting with straightforward, easily resolved issues before heading into thornier ones.

9. Allocate a specific amount of time for each issue. Move through issues, allowing for discussion but discouraging digression or repetition. Use a timer to help monitor the time.

10. Postpone discussion until the end of the meeting if debate on an issue runs overtime. Make sure to cover the other issues on the agenda.

11. Follow up: Circulate copies of the minutes after the meeting to remind everyone of conclusions and action plans.

Tips

To prevent a meeting from going on too long, schedule it before lunch, at the end of the day or immediately before another one.

Try removing the chairs from the meeting room and conducting a stand-up meeting to make it shorter and more efficient.

Things You'll Need

❑ written agenda

❑ visual aids (optional)

❑ timer

32

Take Minutes at a Business Meeting

Business meetings may be conducted formally or informally, depending on the company and the circumstances. These guidelines are based on Robert's Rules of Order.

⊙ Steps

Taking Minutes

1. Obtain the meeting agenda, minutes from the last meeting, and any background documents to be discussed. Consider using a tape recorder to ensure accuracy.

2 Sit beside the chairperson for convenient clarification or help as the meeting proceeds.

3 Write "Minutes of the meeting of [name of committee or association]".

4 Record the date, time and place of the meeting.

5 Circulate a sheet of paper for attendees to sign. (This sheet can also help identify speakers by seating arrangement later in the meeting.) If the meeting is an open one, write down only the names of the attendees who have voting rights.

6 Note who arrives late or leaves early so that these people can be briefed on what they missed.

7 Write down items in the order in which they are discussed. If item 8 on the agenda is discussed before item 2, keep the old item number but write item 8 in second place.

8 Record the motions made and the names of people who originate them.

9 Record whether motions are adopted or rejected, how any vote is taken (by show of hands, voice or other method) and whether such a vote is unanimous. For small meetings, write the names of the attendees who approve, oppose and abstain from each motion.

10 Focus on recording actions taken by the group. Avoid writing down the details of each discussion.

Transcribing Minutes

1 Transcribe minutes soon after the meeting, when your memory is fresh.

2 Follow the format used in previous minutes.

3 Preface resolutions with "RESOLVED, THAT...".

4 Consider attaching long resolutions, reports or other supplementary material to the minutes as an appendix.

5 Write "Submitted by" and then sign your name and the date.

6 Place minutes chronologically in a record book.

Tips

You do not need to record topics irrelevant to the business at hand. Taking minutes is not the same as taking dictation.

Consult only the chairperson, not the attendees, if you have questions.

The person taking minutes does not participate in the meeting.

Write in a concise, accurate manner, taking care not to include subjective opinion.

No matter what type of minutes you take, focus on capturing and communicating all the important actions that took place.

33

Negotiate an Agreement

Whether you are negotiating a business contract or the use of a cubicle, it takes tact and understanding to reach an agreement. Here are some ways to take the sting out of negotiating.

⊙ **Steps**

1   Ask questions to learn what the other side wants. Try to step into the other person's shoes to see the problem from his or her point of view.

2   Communicate what you want. When you speak, make a point instead of just arguing. Focus on understanding and addressing everyone's needs.

3   Summarise conflicts of interest and obstacles to solutions.

4   Break down what you want into specific details so you can search for areas of agreement.

5   Keep talking until you find a solution that meets your mutual interests.

6   If you reach an impasse, end the meeting and reschedule it for another time. A few days of rest might spark some new ideas.

✳ **Tips**

See yourself and the other person as two team members searching for a solution, rather than as opponents.

Stay calm. Nothing is negotiated successfully when both parties are agitated.

Education and Careers

⚠ **Warning**

Avoid taking things personally. When someone is attacking you, he or she is usually just attacking your position.

34

Resolve Conflicts at Work

Friction at work can be stressful and counterproductive for everyone involved. Learn to approach the person with whom you are struggling and resolve the situation.

⊙ Steps

1 Decide whether you want to confront the person who is bothering you. It is usually better to air grievances in the open than to let them fester.

2 Speak to the other person calmly, politely and rationally. Focus on the situation and facts, avoiding gossip and personal attacks.

3 Be careful not to express hostility in your posture, facial expression or tone. Be assertive without being aggressive.

4 Listen to the other person carefully: What is she trying to say? Be sure you understand her position.

5 Express interest in what the other person is saying. It's possible to acknowledge her ideas without necessarily agreeing or submitting. Saying "I understand that you feel this way. Here's how I feel…" acknowledges both positions.

6 Communicate clearly what you want, offering positive suggestions and recommendations. Be willing to be flexible.

7 Speak to your supervisor if a problem with a difficult co-worker seriously threatens your work, but avoid whining.

✳ Tips

Deal with any personality clashes by trying to understand what motivates their behaviour, and then tailoring your actions to work with the personality type. Once you grasp why people behave as they do, you will be able to interact with them more effectively.

For example, be firm with bullies at work – don't let them pressure you into doing anything unwanted. Be forceful in your opinions, but act with a bit of caution.

Around complainers, avoid acting too sympathetically if you feel their complaints are ill-founded – it's better to ask them what sorts of actions they plan to take to change the situation. Squarely ask them what they want.

35

Give a Negative Employee Reference

While it is easy to provide a glowing reference to a former top-notch employee, it is much more challenging to give a negative reference. Here are some simple steps to guide you.

⊙ Steps

1 Confirm to the employer who contacts you that the job candidate worked for your company.

2 State the time period during which the person in question was employed, and his or her job title. Let your personnel department confirm the former employee's salary.

3 Offer no additional information. Derogatory remarks could land you in a costly and lengthy lawsuit.

4 Give the ex-employee a written letter stating the dates of employment and his or her pay level at the time of discharge. This could be presented to prospective employers instead of their having to call you.

5 Inform the ex-employee – if he or she wants to know what you have said – that as a matter of policy you only provide confirmation of employment dates, job title and pay levels.

6 Tell your former employee exactly what you said, if he or she asks you.

*Tip

If the person enquiring about the ex-employee is your close friend, you might be willing to risk making a few general comments about the ex-employee's merits or performance on the job.

⚠ Warning

Remember that anything you say to a prospective employer – even a close friend – could get back to the employee and land you in court.

36

Get Promoted

Promotion is about more than just doing a good job and hoping that your boss notices your huge potential.

⊙ Steps

1   Your biggest clue is in the word "promote". In the workplace, make sure that your strengths and potential are well advertised to colleagues and senior staff.

2   Feel confident that you know every aspect of your current position.

3   Be aware of vacant jobs within your organisation – at the very least, this will show your interest and commitment to the company. Find out as much as you can about any position that interests you.

4   Be seen as smart, punctual and reliable, and willing to take on extra tasks if necessary.

5   Be prepared to work beyond your normal hours if necessary – why would anyone want to promote a "clockwatcher"?

6   Carry out your day-to-day tasks with enthusiasm. It's much easier to get on if you're liked by those around you.

7   Use meetings, conferences and appraisals as opportunities to shine.

*Tip

Take any training opportunities you are offered – it shows that you want to get on. Seek others out for yourself.

⚠ Warning

There's a delicate line between "selling" yourself and outright bragging. Tread that line with care – you don't want to come across as an arrogant git!

37

Ask for a Pay Rise

Consider whether you merit a pay rise and whether your company is in a position to give you one. Then choose your moment and your methods carefully.

⊙ Steps

1 Evaluate your worth. List your achievements, skills and contributions.

2 Arm yourself with information. Know what a normal rise is for someone of your experience and occupation.

3 Assess your superior's mood and outlook. Do you think he or she is ready to consider your request?

4 Choose an appropriate time of day. Make an appointment or ask if there are a few minutes to spare. Plan for an end-of-business-day meeting.

5 Consider asking for a specific amount that's a little higher than you want. Say "eight per cent" when you would be happy with six.

6 Be realistic. If your company is going through tough times but you still feel deserving, decide how you'll respond if a lower amount is offered.

7 Be flexible. Would you consider a supplement in perks, time off, flexible time or holiday time in lieu of a rise? Negotiate.

8 If your superior turns you down, have a back-up plan ready.

✳ Tip

If you can, print out an outline showing that you're paid less than others in your position – but are producing more and better results.

⚠ Warning

Avoid losing your temper or your sense of humour.

Education and Careers

Resign From a Job

Regardless of your reasons for leaving a job, you should do so in a professional manner.

Steps

1 Consider all your options before resigning. Could your employer offer you something that would make you want to stay? Perhaps you should discuss with your employer your dissatisfaction or the better offer that you have received before making a permanent decision.

2 Write a letter of resignation and sign your name. If you were unhappy at the time of leaving, the letter might be a simple sentence conveying the effective date of your resignation. If you were genuinely happy, it could express your regret at leaving and the fact that you'll miss everyone.

3 Refrain from explaining in detail why you are resigning, where you will be working or how much more money you will be making. Do say that you are willing to help with the transition that your resignation will cause.

4 Request a formal meeting with your manager, ideally at the end of the day, so that you can deliver the news in person in addition to giving in the letter. Be sure to close the door.

5 Remember that you can be specific or vague if your supervisor asks for a reason. It's best not to use this time to vent your anger.

6 Stick with the "better opportunity" angle if your tenure was unhappy. If you feel you must tell the truth, try not to be too personal. For example, "I would have preferred more training" is better than "You were terrible at training me".

7 Keep in mind that you may have to get a recommendation from your supervisor, so don't burn your bridges.

Tips

If you would like a letter of recommendation, request one. Have it posted to you.

If you prefer not to say where you're going, a simple "taking time off" will do.

Job Survival

In most cases, a period of notice is expected. This is usually stated in your contract of employment.

Your employer may be angry that you are leaving. Try not to become involved in a dispute about the situation.

⚠ Warning

Be as positive as possible. You might return, or you may later need to ask for a reference. Keep your departure neutral.

39
Survive Redundancy

Losing your job is one of life's most stressful experiences. As more and more companies get "lean and mean", you may find yourself laid off – but you will survive.

◎ Steps

1 Leave your place of work immediately. Even if you saw it coming, you are likely to be too upset to answer questions from colleagues. You can come back later for your coffee mug.

2 Discuss your situation with your spouse and other family members who will be affected. Will your partner have to work overtime for a while? Can your son or daughter get a part-time job to help with college tuition fees?

3 Review your financial situation. You may have set aside what seemed like a reasonable amount for a "rainy day", but if your unemployment goes beyond a month or two, you may need to make some serious lifestyle adjustments.

4 Request a meeting with the company's personnel representative. Find out what redundancy package is being offered, ensure that you are paid for unused holiday, and request details of other relevant aspects, such as dealing with an employment pension or company car.

5 Take advantage of any outplacement services your employer offers. Many companies now provide career assessment and counselling as well as use of company facilities, such as personal computers, copiers and fax machines, to aid redundant employees in their job searches.

6   In most cases, redundancy will entitle you to immediate social security
    allowances. This may be a blow to your self-esteem, but you and your
    family are entitled to such benefits, and meeting basic needs must
    come before pride.

✱ Tips

Get references in writing from your supervisor or personnel manager. Be
sure that any "official" documentation states clearly that your termination
was due to a workforce reduction.

Be sure that when you leave the office you have all the paperwork
necessary for you to claim any statutory benefits.

⚠ Warning

Losing a job – even if through no fault of your own – can be devastating.
If your feelings of anger, sadness or helplessness persist beyond a few
weeks, consider getting short-term therapy for depression.

Going into business for yourself isn't just a matter of opening a bank account and getting some business cards and letterheads printed. When you set up on your own, you'll need to decide what type of business structure to establish for legal and tax purposes. The best structure for your business will depend on various factors, the most important of which are indicated in the table below. (Note, this is intended for initial guidance only. Before you start your business operation, it is essential you consult a solicitor and an accountant.)

chart

	OWNERSHIP RULES	LIABILITY OF OWNERS	CAPITAL	TAXES
Sole Trader	One owner.	Owner is personally liable for all of the business's obligations and debts.	Owner contributes majority of capital with balance from the bank if the business concept looks sound.	Business income, expenses and profit or loss are reported on the owner's annual tax return.
Partnership	Two or more owners working in partnership.	Each partner is liable for all of the business's obligations and debts.	Partners together contribute money or services for a portion of the profits and losses. Banks may provide funding if the project looks sound.	The partnership submits a tax return but the tax is paid by the individual partners.
Limited Liability Partnership	One or more general partners and one or more limited partners.	General partners are liable for all obligations and debts; limited partners have limited liability but do not take part in management.	Partners together contribute money or services for a portion of the profits and losses. Banks may provide funding if the project looks sound.	Similar to a traditional partnership.
Limited Liability Company	Possible to have an unlimited number of shareholders.	Shareholders usually have no personal liability for any of the business's obligations and debts. Directors can be liable in certain situations.	Shareholders will contribute capital by purchasing shares. Banks and venture capitalists (VCs) may provide funding if the project looks sound.	The company is taxed on its earnings. Shareholders are taxed on any dividends they receive. Directors are taxed on their salaries.

Decide Whether to Go Into Business for Yourself

If you want to satisfy your entrepreneurial urge, try owning a small business – but first consider whether your finances, personality and skills are up to the challenge.

⊙ Steps

1 Think about whether you want to work for yourself. Do you enjoy being the boss? Or do you feel more comfortable working for someone else?

2 Determine how much of a risk taker you are. You must be willing to be patient and give the business enough time to get established and grow.

3 Consider how much time and effort goes into running a small business. Many entrepreneurs work harder for themselves than they ever have for a former employer.

4 Find the type of business that suits you. Assess your skills, interests and personal values and seek a business that is in line with these attributes.

5 Decide whether you want to start a business or buy an existing one. Launching a business may involve lower start-up costs, but the business will take time to get established. An existing business usually requires more money up front, but should be less risky.

6 Have enough money in the bank to get started. You'll need enough funds to pay for your everyday living expenses while sustaining the business until it turns a profit. Count on a minimum of three to six months, much more if you want to be a manufacturer.

✳ Tips

Talk to other entrepreneurs to get a perspective on what owning a small business entails.

Visit your local Business Advice Centre – or visit its web pages (businesslink.org) – to learn about any available help to get your business started.

There are many books on starting a business. Learn from others who have already been through the process.

Become Self-Employed

Becoming self-employed – legally this is called "acting as a sole trader" – takes minimal effort. It's also the simplest type of business structure and the easiest to operate.

◉ Steps

1 You can start most businesses right away – with a few important exceptions there is no need for registration or licensing. (Contact your local Council or local Business Advice Centre to find out if you need a license or need to register your particular type of business.)

2 You can trade under your own name. If you want to use a business name you need to comply with the Business Names Act. Contact your local Business Advice Centre or see the Companies House web pages (companieshouse.gov.uk).

3 When you start trading, you must inform the Inland Revenue. If your turnover exceeds a certain threshold you will also need to register for Value Added Tax (VAT) with HM Customs and Excise.

4 Remember to keep receipts for everything you buy in relation to the business, and issue invoices ("bills") to your customers (unless you are a retailer). Keep a record of your business transactions in an accounts book or on a computer accounts program.

5 You can employ staff, but if you do you must inform the Inland Revenue and take responsibility for the deduction of PAYE income tax and National Insurance. The law also requires you to have Employers Liability insurance.

6 Speak to your insurance broker as your domestic and car insurance may be invalidated by your business activities.

✳ Tips

Talk to your local Business Advice Centre (see Yellow Pages or businesslink.org) before you do anything and take advice from a solicitor and accountant.

Use a qualified accountant to help you do your tax returns.

⚠ Warning

Sole traders assume unlimited legal liability with no protection for personal assets if the business goes bankrupt.

43

Form a Partnership

If two or more people work together and no one is an employee then the law regards the arrangement as a "partnership".

⊙ Steps

1 You can start most businesses right away – with a few important exceptions there is no need for registration or licensing. (Contact your local Council or local Business Advice Centre for more information.)

2 If you want to use a business name you need to comply with the Business Names Act. Contact your local Business Advice Centre or see the Companies House web pages (companieshouse.gov.uk).

3 When you start trading, you must inform the Inland Revenue. If your turnover exceeds a certain threshold you will also need to register for Value Added Tax (VAT) with HM Customs and Excise.

4 Keep receipts for everything you buy and sell. Keep a record of your transactions in an accounts book or on a computer accounts program.

5 You can employ staff, but if you do you must inform the Inland Revenue and take responsibility for the deduction of PAYE income tax and National Insurance. The law also requires you to have Employers Liability insurance.

✳ Tip

Although there is no legal requirement, it is recommended you have a Partnership Agreement, which tries to cover issues where disagreements are likely. This will require a solicitor.

Each partner has unlimited legal liability for all the partnership's
obligations and debts, which means your personal assets are at risk if
the business fails owing money.

44

Set Up a Limited Company

A limited company is a legal entity in its own right. It must
have at least one Director and a Company Secretary, who
could be a second Director or another shareholder.

◎ Steps

1   A limited company has to be registered. Contact your solicitor or a
    company registration agent. Only buy from a reputable agent to
    ensure that what you are buying has no existing liabilities. (Companies
    House produces a series of booklets – these are free, or can be read
    online at companieshouse.gov.uk.)

2   Choose a company name that helps you to promote your business,
    but it must not be such that it can be confused with an existing
    company. The Business Names Act applies and in addition a company
    has to have its name on the outside of every place where it carries on
    business.

3   Contact your local Council or local business advice centre to find out
    if you need a license or need to register your particular type of
    business. Failure to obtain such permission may be a criminal offence.
    After you file, the office will let you know if the name has been taken.

4   When you start trading, you must inform the Inland Revenue. If your
    turnover exceeds a certain threshold you will also need to register for
    VAT with HM Customs and Excise.

5   Remember to keep receipts for everything you buy in relation to the
    business, and issue invoices ("bills") to your customers (unless you
    are a retailer). Keep a record of your business transactions in an
    accounts book or on a computer accounts program.

✱ Tips

Ensure your Articles and Memorandum of Association give you plenty of latitude in what the company can do.

Use a qualified accountant to help you do your tax returns.

⚠ Warning

Limited liability does not mean no liability. Directors can be held personally liable if the company trades fraudulently or they ignore their legal responsibilities.

45

Research the Market for Your Product or Service

Before you start your business, test the market to make sure there will be demand for your product or service.

◎ Steps

1 Learn about your market. Go to trade shows and network with other professionals in your line of business. Subscribe to trade publications.

2 Spend time with potential customers. Ask friends and acquaintances what they'd like in the type of product or service you want to sell.

3 Set up a focus group to gather opinions about your product or service. This could be a gathering of friends, or a more formal group assembled by a market research firm. Be sure to get reactions to your likely prices.

4 Send out a survey to potential customers. Make the form easy to fill in by asking multiple-choice questions. Ask the respondents if they would buy this product or service. Keep the survey short and enclose a stamped addressed envelope.

5 Analyse your findings to determine whether your idea is viable. How did people react to your product or service? What do people like or dislike about your product or service? Make adjustments, including the hardest one – letting go of your idea, if necessary, and finding another one.

✱ Tips

Make sure that the people you're surveying are indeed those who are potential customers.

Collect a large sample so that your findings will be accurate.

Create a well-designed survey. Ask very specific questions.

⚠ Warnings

Don't assume that what you like is what others will like. You must meet the needs of the greatest number of customers.

Be brutally honest with yourself – be prepared to accept that there may be insufficient demand for your idea.

46

Write a Business Plan

Every business should have a business plan. It is your road map to the future and is usually essential if you want to get finance.

⊙ Steps

1 Collect the information for your business plan. Include information on your business, product or service, customers, market, competition and potential risks.

2 Write a summary. This is the first section of the plan – a single-page description of all the elements covered in more detail later.

3 Describe your business. Spell out the purpose of your business plan. Talk about the skills you and your management team have.

4 Explain your product or service. Detail how you will make or provide it. Analyse the costs associated with this process. List your supply sources.

5 Talk about the market you're entering. Discuss general trends in the industry. Include details about the market segment you are pursuing, the niche you are targeting and your target customer; provide

demographics on your potential customers and explain their buying habits. Analyse your competition. Be realistic.

6 Describe your marketing plan. Explain how you will generate sales through advertising, promotion and public relations. Estimate all costs conservatively.

7 Detail your yearly revenue projections and your expenses using a cashflow forecast.

✳ Tip

Gather all the information for your business plan before you start writing it. Limit the plan to about 10 to 20 pages (more for a major venture). Investors and lenders get business plans every day – most get a cursory look before they are either discarded or kept for further review.

⚠ Warning

A business plan is a never-ending process. As your business grows, update your business plan projections.

47

Do a Cashflow Forecast

Plan, raise finance and manage your business successfully using a cash-flow forecast.

⊙ Steps

1 Use a spreadsheet program to help you create your cashflow forecast. Each horizontal row is for a specific category of "Cash In" or "Cash Out" which is listed in the first vertical column. Under "Cash In", there should be rows for "Sales", "Capital" and "Loans". Under "Cash Out" will be the categories of expenses relevant to your business.

2 Each subsequent column represents a month. Forecast for 12 months ahead, ending with a "Totals" column. Fill in the 12 months of figures – these are almost all estimates at this stage.

3 Ensure the figures are balanced – if you are selling a product where the typical mark-up is 100%, then your "Stock" line should run at

about half that of your "Sales" line, otherwise you will be either run out of stock or find yourself overstocked.

4   Try different "what if" scenarios. In this way you can begin to see how much capital your business requires, sales targets you need to achieve, and where you are most vulnerable.

5   Update your cashflow forecast monthly to ensure you are running on track.

✱ Tips

Always be pessimistic about likely sales. Furthermore, allow time (at least six months for a service business – much more for a manufacturing business) before forecast sales reach a reasonable level.

Never underestimate your projected overheads.

⚠ Warning

Never confuse cash inflow with profitability. Remember, the bottom line of a cashflow forecast does not represent either a "profit" or a "loss".

48
Hire Employees

A business is only as good as the people it employs.

⊙ Steps

1   Determine what jobs you need done and what skills are needed.

2   Write precise job descriptions, including duties and skill requirements.

3   Conduct salary surveys among similar businesses in comparable locations to determine how much to budget for salaries.

4   Advertise in appropriate media. If you need general staff, advertise in local newspapers. If you need specialists, consider trade publications or other specialised media, including job fairs and the internet.

5   Interview carefully. Focus on the applicant's qualifications, track record, attitude and demeanour. Why did they leave their previous jobs?

6 Bring others into the interview process. Ask the applicant to meet others in your business so that you can get others' impressions.

7 Check references and employment history.

8 Put your offer in writing, spelling out the job description, hours, salary, benefits, holiday and other pertinent details. get your solicitor to check your offer letter.

Tips

Create an annual employee budget to know how much you can afford.

Let current employees know about openings that might be of interest to them.

Make sure the job description is accurate, so people will know what they are applying for.

⚠ Warning

It is unlawful for an employer to discriminate on grounds of gender, race or disability.

49

Write a Mission Statement

Writing a mission statement will help you and your employees focus on a common goal and give everyone a benchmark to gauge performance.

◎ Steps

1 Include everybody whose perception of your business matters. Collect as many ideas as you can.

2 Define your business. Think carefully about what role it plays in the industry and community.

3 State the things to which you're dedicated. Are you dedicated to quality, your customers, your success?

4 Assess the value of your product or service. Use written questionnaires to survey your customers, suppliers, partners and other external parties about the benefits of and ideals behind your business.

5 Set up a small committee to go through the ideas you have collected and incorporate them into your mission statement.

6 Give the mission statement high visibility; hang a copy in your work area. People will see it every day and be reminded of what their work means.

Tip

Live your mission statement every day. In order to gain credibility with your employees, customers and suppliers, you must practise what you preach.

⚠ Warning

Be realistic. Set standards that are reasonable and attainable by you and your employees.

50

Apply for a Business Loan

Money to expand a business can come from a variety of sources. Most require you to provide a thorough financial profile.

⊙ Steps

1 Question yourself carefully about the loan: What is it for? How much do you need? When do you need it?

2 Decide on the type of loan you want and whether you want to obtain it from a bank or another lender.

3 Update the balance sheet so that it reflects the current status of assets, liabilities and ownership.

4 Update the profit-and-loss statement with a summary covering business expenses, revenues and costs for a recent accounting period.

5 Develop cashflow projections for at least one year, showing how money will flow in and out of the business quarter by quarter.

6 Combine all of the above information into a business plan – this is the key document a lender will review (see 46 "Write a Business Plan").

7 Have your solicitor review any loan offer, documents or stipulations.

✳ Tips

If two banks turn you down for a loan, your application may be unconvincing.

Apply for finance well before you actually need the money.

Owners with few business assets can expect to put up personal assets to secure a loan.

⚠ Warning

Be wary of lenders that want to secure your intellectual property or excessive assets as collateral for your loan.

51
Secure Venture Capital Money

Venture capitalists (VCs) invest money in major start-ups in exchange for equity shareholding in the company. VCs receive hundreds of applications from entrepreneurs each year. Here's how to stand out.

◎ Steps

1 Prepare a business plan. VCs will expect you to clearly define the purpose of your business, disclose pertinent financial information (including revenue streams and projections) and provide information on your executive management team.

2 Do internet research on venture funds and contact your local Business Advice Centre to find the appropriate fit for your company. Some VCs focus on retail and service companies, while others look specifically for technology start-ups.

3 Try to get a personal introduction to a VC rather than sending out your business plan. Introductions can be made by executives of companies already being funded by the VC or by lawyers and accountants who work with the firm. Try to contact four to five VCs.

4   Arrange a meeting with the VC. Consider bringing key members of the management team to the meeting.

5   Follow up your visit with a thank-you note and additional information.

6   Be persistent and polite.

✳ Tips

VCs want to see that you've done the basic groundwork and are ready to springboard to the next level. Spell out your next big step, and the resources you will need to get there. Investors want to see that you have a vision for your company and that you have plans to grow and expand.

Show off your top executive team. VCs want to see a solid management team which is knowledgeable, flexible, driven and committed.

⚠ Warnings

Acquiring funding is a demanding process – you'll need a thick skin, patience and determination.

VCs can be greedy – don't give too much equity away.

52

Bring Your Business Online

Going online requires a strong business model and a sense of what you want to accomplish by having a website.

◉ Steps

1   Decide whether your web pages are simply to provide information about your business or to transact online sales. Answering such questions can help determine the amount of effort required to build the site.

2   Decide if you are going to develop your own web pages or have them designed by a professional. (Use a developer unless you are an expert.)

3   Gather information on web publishing via books, magazines and other current periodicals.

4   Browse other web pages for design and functionality ideas – good and bad.

Business

5   Apply for a domain name.

6   Begin to develop the site. Install various checkpoints along the way
    to ensure that the project is progressing in the right direction.

7   Implement your marketing campaign before your site goes live, and
    step up your marketing efforts to bring traffic to your site after. (Be
    aware that it can take many months before search engines list your
    site.)

✳Tips

When registering for a domain name, think of alternative names in case
your first choice is taken.

If you have a smaller business, consider selling your products through
online classifieds and/or online auctions. These are simpler and less
expensive ways of transacting commerce online.

⚠Warnings

Begin planning as soon as you decide you want a site.

Don't automatically assume that your web pages will generate sufficient
business to cover the costs of the site.

53

Apply for a Patent

A patent gives you the exclusive right (for a limited period) to
make, use or sell a product or process that you have
invented. The process of applying requires professional
assistance and the costs can be considerable. If renewed
annually a patent can last up to 20 years but is a territorial
right – a UK patent is only effective within the UK. Applying for
foreign patents involves further paperwork and expense.

⊙Steps

1   Determine if your idea warrants patent protection. For more useful
    information, look at the Patent Office's web page (patent.gov.uk).

2   To be patentable, your invention must meet four key criteria:

(i) Be new – anywhere in the world.

(ii) Involve an inventive step which would not be obvious to an expert in the field.

(iii) Be capable of industrial application – i.e. be such that it can be made or used.

iv) Not be one of a number specifically excluded categories. (These include: discoveries, scientific theories; aesthetic creations; literary or artistic works; computer programs.)

3   If you think you have an invention that is patentable, you should not publicly disclose the invention before you apply for a patent. Any such disclosure – by word-of-mouth, demonstration, advertisement or article in a publication – could prevent the patent being granted.

4   In the UK, only a tiny minority of patents are by private individuals, the remainder are filed by companies, universities and government research agencies. Most private inventors find that their biggest challenge is getting their invention into production so they can earn something from their patent.

5   Once granted a patent can itself be bought or sold.

 Tip

The grant of a patent should not be taken as any indication that your invention has any commercial value. Most don't!

⚠ Warning

This information is by no means a substitute for professional advice. Refer to a qualified patent agent at a very early stage of your project and prior to any public disclosure.

54

Decide if a Home-Based Business Is Right for You

Working from home sounds like the ideal way to work, but your personality, lifestyle and home life will dictate whether it is a viable alternative for you.

⊙ Steps

1   Ask yourself what you are trying to accomplish by starting a home-based business. Do you want more time to spend with your family? Do you want to have some flexibility in your work hours? Do you want to be your own boss? Do you want to make more money?

2   Consider your personality when making this decision. Are you the sort of person who enjoys the solitude of working alone?

3   Consider whether there are small children, pets or anything else that might distract you at home.

4   Decide what type of business you are interested in. Is it performing a service or creating a product? Is it best done at home, or will an office or additional workspace be required once you are successful?

5   Talk to other people who do the same or similar work from home. Ask what problems they run into.

6   Discover whether you can make enough money to meet your financial needs doing this sort of work.

7   Research what sort of resources will be required to get your business going – space, cash, equipment, marketing.

8   Can you do all the work yourself or will this business will require work from additional people? Can you use sub-contractors or will you have to hire employees? (The latter may be a problem in a home environment.)

9   Decide on a type of business that suits your personal needs and meets your financial commitments.

10   Get legal advice on any legal or planning constraints to using your home for business purposes.

✱ Tip

Ask yourself these key lifestyle/ workstyle questions: Are you a self-starter? Can you meet deadlines without someone constantly reminding you? Do you need personal interaction throughout the day? Can you make decisions on your own? Do you enjoy having lunch with co-workers? Do you need a regimented workday? Do you prefer to leave your work behind when you leave the office? Do you prefer a flexible schedule that allows you to intersperse personal needs with work needs?

Running a Small Business

⚠ Warnings

Running a home-based business is not glamorous; it is hard work, requiring great time management and dedication.

Although working from home makes it easier to do things around the house, you might very well find yourself caught in a vice when family and work demands conflict.

55

Set Up a Home Office

Once you're ready to set up shop in your home, it's time to turn that spare room or little corner into your office.

◉ Steps

1 Establish a permanent space within your home for your office. If you have the space, a separate room is best.

2 Decide on an office arrangement. The best is a U-shaped arrangement, which lets you use three surfaces to keep everything within reach.

3 Choose an L-shaped arrangement that provides a secondary surface if space is limited. An alternative is a parallel arrangement which can provide two full-sized working surfaces if they are placed opposite one another.

4 Consider a V-shaped arrangement, which consists of a small working area in front of you (generally used for a computer monitor) and two surfaces angled to your left and right if your office area is very small.

5 Establish two phone lines – one for voice and one for fax and/or internet – or broadband for your office. If you'll need to forward calls to other offices, ask your phone company about related services.

6 Buy office furniture that suits the arrangement you've chosen. Include desks and tables, chairs and desk lamps.

7 Buy a phone with a built-in answering machine and a hold button. If you'll be transferring calls from within your home office, make sure your phone has a transfer button.

8   Buy a computer system, including a printer and perhaps a scanner. Consider built-in fax software if you'll be sending and receiving files created on a PC. Buy a separate fax machine if necessary. To save money, buy a fax machine that also serves as a scanner and photocopier.

9   Stock your office with standard office supplies. If you're self-employed, budget the cost of these items in your monthly business expenses; otherwise, your employer may provide these supplies for you.

✳ Tips

If you don't have a separate room available, use devices like screens, bookcases and directed lighting to create the necessary separation between home space and office space.

Things You'll Need

❑ desk

❑ desk chair

❑ desk lamp

❑ phone lines

❑ telephone

❑ answering machine

❑ internet access and broadband

❑ computer

❑ printer

❑ fax modem or fax machine/copier

❑ office supplies

56

Reduce Expenses in a Home-Based Business

Working from home is much less costly than renting office space. Once you've decided to forgo the hassle and expense of commuting, there are additional ways to reduce your costs.

1 Keep complete and accurate accounting records, and review your expenses every few months to determine where you could cut back.

2 Purchase multi-function office machines. For example, look for a fax machine that also copies and scans documents.

3 Set the costs of business use of your vehicle and home against tax. Keep all your receipts

4 Earn supplier discounts. Sometimes a supplier may offer a small discount if an invoice is paid quickly.

5 Give free internet access services a try (see 83 "Evaluate Free Internet Service Providers").

6 Go over your insurance coverage with your insurance broker and look for ways to cut your premiums. Consider adding an incidental business option to your existing homeowner's insurance at a much lower cost than a standard business liability policy.

7 Check garage sales, classified ads or internet auctions for cheap office furniture. You can get great bargains, and sometimes you can even find like-new used or reconditioned fax machines and computers.

8 Shut off non-essential equipment at night.

✱ **Tip**

Consult an accountant before applying for tax deductions for business use of your home and vehicle.

⚠ **Warning**

Don't get too budget-happy and stop buying items that are truly necessary to your operation, such as trade journals and training courses.

57
Buy a Computer

Buying a computer means investigating its different features: RAM (random-access memory), processor speed, graphics capability, hard disk space and so on. Here's how to start.

Computers

⊙ Steps

1 Before you start shopping, decide which features you'll need based on what you're planning to do with the computer. For example, if you're going to be creating graphics, sound and video, you'll want plenty of RAM. If you're going to be doing heavy computational tasks (searching large databases, watching video), you'll want a faster processor.

2 Decide which "platform" you want to use: the most common two are PC and Apple Macintosh.

3 Decide if you want a laptop computer, which you can carry around with you, or a desktop model.

4 Choose a computer brand based on quality, price and technical support.

5 Work out the core configuration you need, including processor and speed, amount of RAM and hard disk capacity.

6 Determine which additional types of drive you need, such as CD-ROM, DVD-ROM, CD/DVD recorder or Zip.

7 Select any necessary peripheral hardware devices, such as printer, scanner, modem, sound cards, video cards and speakers, and decide how many extra internal card slots and disk drive bays you'll need in order to allow room for future expansion.

8 Determine any pre-installed software you may need. For example, an operating system – Windows or the Mac OS – an anti-virus program and software for word processing, spreadsheets and databases.

9 Choose the warranty or service coverage appropriate to your needs.

10 Buy from a computer specialist, retail chain, consumer electronics shop, discount chain, or mail-order/online retailer. Buy when you need to buy. No matter how long you wait for the best deal, the same – or better – configuration will cost less in a few months.

✳ Tips

Keep abreast of the latest technology by reading the new-product reviews in magazines and on the web.

Find out which hardware and software are included with the models you're considering, and use that as a basis for comparing prices. Ask "What's the catch?" if a price seems too low.

Computer Equipment

Understand that RAM is where your computer temporarily stores data to be processed. Although more RAM is better, you don't necessarily need much if you restrict your computer use to simple tasks such as sending e-mails or word processing. Games, however, can require lots of RAM; graphics and sound are other space hogs.

The processors found on most modern computers are usually fast enough for all but the most demanding applications, such as streaming video.

58
Buy Peripherals for a Computer

You need a monitor, keyboard and mouse to use a computer. What other peripherals are worth considering?

⊙ **Steps**

1   You will need a printer – unless you have access to one at work or plan to use your computer only to surf the internet. Ink-jet printers cost less and can print colours. Laser printers are more expensive (only very expensive ones can print in colour) but have better text quality and are more likely to print industry-standard PostScript fonts. Laser printers cost less per use, as ink-jet cartridges run out quickly and are expensive. (See 63 "Buy a Laser Printer").

2   Buy a scanner if you want to "photocopy" text, documents or pictures into your computer.

3   Buy a back up storage device, such as an external hard drive, Zip drive or CD-RW drive, if you need to back up large amounts of data and your computer doesn't have a suitable built-in drives.

4   If your system came with unpowered speakers, buy a pair of powered stand-alone speakers for better sound quality and higher output .

5   Buy a microphone to record your own sounds, or to use computer telephony, voice activation and various educational programs.

6   A digital camera is the easiest way of transferring photographs into your computer (see 61 "Choose a Digital Camera").

7 Buy other peripherals to meet specific wants and needs. For example, buy a joystick to increase your speed and flexibility when playing action games, or a digital video camera for teleconferencing (see 62 "Choose a web Camera").

✱ Tip
Manufacturers introduce new types of peripherals all the time. Something not even invented when you buy your computer might well increase its capability later on.

⚠ Warning
Ensure that your computer is capable of meeting the minimum system requirements of any peripherals you buy.

59

Buy a Computer Monitor

The main criteria for selecting a monitor are size and resolution (the ability to render detail). If you work with graphics or play computer games, you'll need a monitor with higher resolution.

◉ Steps

1 Determine how big a monitor will fit on your desk. If desk space is limited, consider buying a flat-screen monitor.

2 Even if ultimately you buy from a mail-order or web retailer, visit a local computer store to check out different monitors in person.

3 Compare features such as anti-glare coating, digital controls, built-in microphone, built-in speakers or speaker mounts, USB ports and ease of adjustment.

4 Compare limited warranties.

5 Make your buying decision based on display clarity in the size you want, for the price you want to pay.

✳ Tips

For gaming or graphics, look for a refresh rate of at least 75 Hz at 1,024 by 768 resolution.

Ensure that your graphics card meets the monitor's maximum specs for refresh rate and resolution.

⚠ Warning

The tube size and viewable area of a monitor are not the same. Read system specs carefully.

60

Get the Best Price on Computer Software

Price variations on software from retail stores and internet retailers are small, but you can get free programs legally, or find other ways to save. Here are some options to explore.

◎ Steps

1 Use internet search engines that find the best price on specific products.

2 Get software free from your employer. Many businesses purchase multicomputer licences and are only too happy to have you work from home.

3 If you will be using the software for a home-based business, ask a large retailer for a business price.

4 Buy a "works" program (one program with various functions) or an office suite (a set of related programs) instead of individual word processing, spreadsheet and database programs if you plan on using most or all of the programs.

5 Buy the upgrade version of Microsoft Office instead of the full version if you already have any of these programs: all office suites, Microsoft Works, WordPerfect, Lotus 1-2-3 or any Microsoft program included in the version of Office you want.

Computers

6   If you don't need sophisticated features, consider shareware or
    freeware programs or buy a basic program instead of a professional
    version. Search the internet for programs of the type you want.

7   If you don't need new features, you can usually buy older versions of
    a program at a hugely discounted price after an update has been
    released. If you change your mind, you can often upgrade
    inexpensively.

✴ Tips

Be aware that most software manufacturers offer upgrade prices to
users of competing software.

Most chain retailers will give you a price adjustment (usually between
100 and 150 per cent of the difference) if the price of a product is
reduced (by that store or a local competitor) within a week or two of
purchase.

⚠ Warning

Remember to add shipping costs when comparing prices from internet
and other mail-order retailers.

61

Choose a Digital Camera

Digital cameras offer the convenience of immediate viewing,
multiple-image storage and computer connectivity – and
there's no film to develop.

◉ Steps

1   Buy the camera with the highest resolution you can afford. At least 3
    megapixels (3 million pixels) are needed for professional results.

2   Look for a 100-per cent glass lens as opposed to a plastic one.

3   Most digital cameras store images on removable RAM cards, such as
    the Compact Flash format; the larger the capacity, the less frequently
    you'll need to download or erase your photographs.

4   Expect zoom to be the feature you will use most. Compare optical, as
    opposed to digital, zoom capabilities.

Computer Equipment

5 Compare the different flash modes.

6 Investigate viewfinders: Look for an optical (through-the-lens) viewfinder as well as an LCD display.

7 Consider autofocus and macro features, shutter-release lag times, and bundled software.

8 Compare additional features you might want, such as interchangeable lenses, steady-shot, burst mode, auto exposure, variable shutter speeds, automatic white balance, voice memo, manual focus and self-timer.

9 Compare removable media of various types (if you need more storage space for your photographs).

10 Investigate batteries, chargers and AC adaptor units.

11 Look for additional features, such as USB or FireWire connectivity (to connect the camera to your computer) or a battery-status indicator. As well as video connections for looking at your pictures on a TV screen.

❋ Tips

If you will only output pictures to a computer monitor (for viewing, web-page use or e-mail), an inexpensive digital camera with a 640-by-480-pixel resolution will provide satisfactory results.

If you plan to print photographs on a good (at least 720 dots per inch) colour printer, look for a high-resolution camera.

A 2-megapixel camera will be able to provide photo-quality output for 13- by 18-cm (5- by 7-in) prints.

⚠ Warnings

Watch out for high-resolution cameras at bargain prices. The resolution claimed may only apply to software interpolation, rather than true optical resolution.

If you do buy a cheap camera, make sure that it has a charge-coupled device (CCD).

Computers

Choose a Web Camera

Web cameras (webcams) stream live video or frequently
changing still images onto web pages. The most commonly
used type – a videoconferencing camera – is discussed here.

⊙ Steps

1 Try to get the highest frame-per-second rate, highest resolution and
best fidelity you can.

2 Compare lens types and focus controls.

3 Consider camera sizes and mounting options. Most cameras will sit
on top of a monitor, but not all rotate both horizontally and vertically.

4 Compare bundled software and the manufacturers' limited warranties
(most run for one year).

5 Check for additional features, such as a zoom or telephoto lens, video
still-capture quality and a built-in microphone.

✴ Tips

You can also use a digital still camera or a digital camcorder as a
webcam.

Make sure your computer has an appropriate port for connecting the
camera. USB is the most common interface standard.

⚠ Warning

Windows NT does not support USB.

63

Buy a Laser Printer

For most uses, laser printers provide better quality than ink-jet
printers. However, they also cost more. Consider print quality,
speed, reliability and price.

Computer Equipment

⊙ Steps

1   Decide what types of documents you want to print – text, graphics, non-standard paper sizes, for example.

2   List specific needs, such as the ability to handle large files, printing on different types of media (labels, envelopes) without jamming, the number of paper trays, and compatibility with specific software.

3   Compare the print quality of different printers. Compare the resolution, or dpi (dots per inch). Use a magnifying glass if print quality is critical.

4   Compare speed specifications. Although you may not achieve the rated speed in a domestic setting, it is useful for comparing printers.

5   Learn how much RAM the printers have, and whether it's expandable.

6   Understand that the printer's paper path needs to be no sharper than 90 degrees to consistently handle envelopes, labels, transparencies or card stock. If you plan to use special media often, avoid printers with 180-degree U-turn paper paths.

7   Compare prices of consumable items such as toner cartridges and replacement drums.

8   Compare warranties and service contracts.

✳ Tips

Look for at least 600-by-600 dpi (dots per inch) resolution.

If you want to print PostScript fonts or graphics, you'll need a PostScript printer. Many – although not all – laser printers can cope with PostScript; most ink-jet printers can't.

Printer RAM will affect the speed of the printer and its ability to handle large files. If the printer includes many built-in fonts, that may also improve speed.

You may need to purchase the printer cable separately.

⚠ Warning

Be wary of "laser-class" printers. These inexpensive printers use toner cartridges, but use LEDs instead of lasers and produce inferior text quality.

Computers

Buy a Laptop Computer

A laptop computer is no real substitute for a desktop computer, but a good laptop can be a solid and convenient supplement to a desktop model.

⊙Steps

1 Check out the periodic surveys in leading computer and technology magazines for comprehensive information on the reliability of specific laptop brands. (Customer satisfaction ratings are a good indicator.) Make your choice based on quality, price and limited warranty.

2 Determine the core configuration you need, including processor and speed, amount of RAM, and hard disk size.

3 Decide on the type of display. Choose a dual-scan display if your budget is extremely limited. Select an active-matrix display for the quickest response and best visual quality, though at the cost of shorter battery life. Choose an HPA (High-Performance Addressing) display if your budget rules out an active-matrix display but you need to use the laptop under difficult lighting and wish to maximise battery life.

4 Compare weights of units you're considering. Think about how often and how far you'll need to carry the computer and its peripherals.

5 Determine the size of display you want. Remember that bigger screens add to the unit's price, weight and bulk.

6 Choose an ultraportable unit if weight is more important than price, reliability, battery life and ease of use.

7 Buy a unit with built-in CD-ROM or other drives if convenience is more important than portability or reliability. Consider a model with removable drives for the most flexibility.

8 Test the comfort and feel of the input device and keyboard. Choose between a touch pad, used by most manufacturers, and the pointing stick (also called the "command point") used by IBM and Toshiba.

9 Make sure the laptop comes with a lithium-ion battery. Be sceptical of manufacturers' battery-life claims.

10 Decide what pre-installed software you want or need.

11 Choose the length of warranty or service coverage you need.

Tips

Touch pads are more reliable than pointing sticks.

Get a laptop with a DVD-ROM drive if you would like to watch films while travelling.

Consider leasing a computer if you need to upgrade often or spread out payments over two or more years. Keep in mind, however, that leasing is always more expensive than buying.

65

Get the Best Battery Life From a Laptop Computer

A rechargeable battery will last an average of two years. You can, however, take steps to get a better total battery life and longer battery life per charge.

⊙ Steps

1 Charge the battery for 12 hours before use.

2 Let the battery drain completely before recharging if you have a nickel-cadmium (NiCad) battery. Upgrade to a nickel-metal-hydride (NiMH) battery – or better, a lithium-ion battery – if one is made for your machine.

3 Let the battery drain as much as possible before recharging if you have an NiMH battery.

4 Recharge an NiMH battery between long periods of inactivity.

5 Travel with an extra battery. Use the two batteries equally.

6 If you can, avoid running floppy, Zip, CD or DVD drives off the battery.

7 Reduce the display's brightness when possible.

Tips

As time goes by, you will need to recharge any rechargeable battery more frequently. When the battery life is less than 25 per cent of its original

Computers

level, it's probably time to get a new battery. (With normal use, expect about half the per-charge life claimed by the manufacturer.)

Only use power-management software in those instances when you can sacrifice performance for battery life.

If you're buying a laptop, get one with a lithium-ion battery.

66

Travel With a Laptop

Protecting your laptop from theft and damage, and ensuring that it can be used in foreign countries, requires preparation and care.

⊙ Steps

1 Get a heavily padded carrying case that will hold the peripherals and accessories you need to carry.

2 To deter theft, use a case that isn't obviously for a laptop.

3 Take the components, peripherals and accessories you might need, but leave the CD-ROM drive or other parts you won't. Take an extra fully charged battery if you intend using the laptop on a long journey.

4 Remove disks from disk drives.

5 Ensure that you have any power and telephone adaptors necessary for use abroad. Find out the power requirements and plug shapes for your destination before you leave.

6 Find out what communication facilities will be available. Learn in advance how you can connect to your ISP if necessary

7 Back up all important documents before you leave.

8 Check your insurance and warranty cover.

9 Make sure your laptop has enough battery power to boot up if required by customs or security personnel.

10 Avoid leaving your computer unattended in the airport.

11 Deter theft and breakage by monitoring your laptop closely as it travels through the x-ray machine. Better yet, ask for a manual inspection.

12 Keep your laptop out of overhead bins and in plain sight when flying.

13 Once you arrive, change the date and time settings and – if necessary – the modem settings.

✱ Tip

An airport X-ray machine won't erase your data, but a metal detector can.

⚠ Warning

Do not plug your laptop directly into a foreign outlet, even if you have an adaptor plug – or you may fry your computer. Always use a power converter that claims it can handle the voltage at your destination. (Make sure it can handle your computer's current draw as well.)

Things You'll Need

☐ carrying case

☐ extra battery (optional)

☐ adaptor plug(s) and power converter (optional)

☐ telephone adaptors (optional)

67
Learn to Type

Mastering a computer keyboard isn't that difficult if you go about it methodically and practice a little every day. Here are some basic steps to get you started.

⊙ Steps

1 Put your fingers on the "home row": left little finger on *a*, left third finger finger on *s*, left middle finger on *d*, and left index finger on *f*. For the right hand, put the little finger on the semicolon, the third finger on *l*, the middle finger on *k*, and the index finger on *j*.

2 Type the following letters – looking anywhere but the keyboard – saying the names of the letters out loud and using either thumb to hit the space bar: *f f space j j space d d space k k space s s space l l space a a space semicolon semicolon space.*

3   Repeat this as many times as you need to in order to feel that you're getting an intuitive sense of these letters.

4   Bring in *g* and *h* by reaching with the appropriate index finger.

5   Use this same talking-out-loud technique to learn the rows above and below the home row: the left little finger for *q* and *z*; the right little finger for *p* and the slash. Again, the index fingers do double duty: *r, t, v* and *b* for the left index finger; *u, y, m* and *n* for the right index finger.

6   Use your little fingers for the shift key: the left when the right hand is typing the letter and vice versa.

7   Learn the numbers: left little finger for *1*, left index finger for *4* and *5*, right little finger for *0*, and right index finger for *6* and *7*.

8   Move to actual texts as soon as you can, since they'll make your learning real.

9   Master other keys as you see fit – such as the Control key and the arrow keys – but be aware that these differ from keyboard to keyboard and may not be worth learning.

10 Practice for at least 15 to 30 minutes every day.

✳ Tips

Consider taking a a typing class or using instructional software if you feel you would learn better from a structured course.

Some find the number keys too far away to type accurately. If you experience this, watch these keys as you type, since errors with numbers can be costly.

If you use a word-processing program, check the reference manual or Help menu to learn about formatting techniques, such as changing the type style and setting new margins.

⚠ Warnings

However tempting it may be, avoid looking at the keyboard – it really is the only way to learn to type.

Although the letters always remain the same, some of the other character keys may vary slightly on different models of computer keyboard.

Back Up a Hard Drive

It's important to make frequent back ups of critical files. The following explains how to run Microsoft's built-in Backup utility in the Windows operating system (from Windows 95 onwards).

Steps

1   Connect a drive (such as a Zip drive or other removable media, a tape drive or a second hard disk drive) that can hold the information you want to back up.

2   Open the Start menu and select Programs.

3   In the submenu that appears, click Accessories, then System Tools.

4   Click Backup to run Microsoft's Backup program.

5   For the easiest back up, answer the questions presented to you by the Backup Wizard. (The wizard will ask you what you want to back up, where you want to store the back up, if you want the data to be verified and/or compressed, and what you want to name the back up.)

6   Click Next after you answer each question.

7   Click Start to commence the back up.

✳ Tips

If you don't have a large-capacity backup drive, it may be more convenient to save a limited number of critical files, not your entire hard disk. You can also back up files to a network drive.

To restore a disk from a back up, open the Tools menu in the Backup utility. Select Restore Wizard.

⚠ Warning

Microsoft Backup cannot be used to write to CD-R/CD-RW. However, this can be done with add-on software.

Computers

Exit a "Frozen" Windows Program

When a program freezes, you can't work in it or exit from it. You're trapped! But not if you follow these instructions, which work for Windows (from Windows 95 onwards).

⊙ Steps

1 Use the keyboard command Control+Alt+Delete, pressing the keys simultaneously. A box labelled Close Programs appears.

2 Scroll through the list of open programs until you come to the one that has frozen.

3 Select the frozen program.

4 Click on End Task.

5 A message will appear saying, "Program is not responding. End task?" Click on End Task. The program will shut down, and you'll be able to reopen it in the usual way.

✱ Tips

Using the command Control-Alt-Delete twice in a row will shut down the computer.

If your programs keep freezing, restart the computer.

△ Warning

When a program freezes, any unsaved material may be lost. Some applications may allow you to recover some material lost in a crash.

Uninstall a Windows Program Safely

When you install a program, it usually includes additional files scattered throughout your Windows folder. To remove a program completely, use the Add/Remove Programs utility.

1 Check your documentation to see if the application has its own custom uninstall program, and use it if it's available.

2 If not, open the Start menu and select Settings, then Control Panel.

3 Double-click on Add/Remove Programs.

4 Find the program you want, then click Add/Remove.

5 In the box that appears, confirm to remove the program and click through the Wizard that follows.

6 Consider using a third-party utility, such as Clean Sweep or Norton Utilities, to uninstall remnants of programs from your system.

✳ Tips

The Add/Remove Programs utility will normally alert you to the presence of shared programs and allow you to leave them on your system.

Only delete an application folder as a last resort. The program could have added programs or files to additional folders. To be safe, rename the application folder and reboot your PC. If it restarts without a problem, delete the folder. If it does not, rename the folder with its original name and do not delete it.

71

Troubleshoot a Computer

Is your computer functioning strangely or – worse still – not at all? Before paying for technical support, look at your system. A little common sense may help you solve simple problems.

⊙ Steps

1 Restart the computer. Some software problems will correct themselves when you do this.

2 Check your cables. Keyboard not working? Make sure it's plugged in. Mouse not responding? Make sure it's plugged in.

3 Check the electric power. Test the socket by plugging a lamp into the same power source as your computer.

4   Disconnect peripheral devices (such as a printer or external drive) and restart the computer.

5   Consider the possibility of a computer virus. Run an anti-virus program (see 80 "Protect a Computer From Viruses").

6   Run a utility program (such as Norton Disk Doctor) to defragment your hard drive or to identify and fix certain problems.

 Tips

If you do decide to call technical support, write down the exact problem and what you were doing when it occurred. Also note any error messages.

Be as specific as possible when talking to the support person.

Computers tend to crash or hang when their hard disks become too full. Try to free up space by deleting any unnecessary files and emptying the Trash or Recycle Bin.

72

Start Your Windows Computer in DOS

Installation instructions for some older DOS games and other applications require you to boot to MS-DOS. Troubleshooting in Windows may also require this.

◎ **Steps**

1   Click Start.

2   Click Shut Down.

3   In the box that appears, click Restart in MS-DOS mode.

4   Click OK.

 Tips

Type "exit" and press Enter to return to Windows from MS-DOS.

DOS can also be opened in the Start menu and selecting Programs, then MS-DOS Prompt.

73

Change Your Default Printer

You can change the default printer to any other printer that is connected to your computer. These instructions are for the Windows 95/98/NT operating systems.

⊙ Steps

1 Click on the Start menu and click on Settings, then Printers.

2 A window will appear showing the icons of all the printers that are installed on your system. Right-click on the icon for the printer you want to use as the default. A menu will appear.

3 Click on Set as Default.

4 To make sure the correct printer is now set as the default, right-click on the printer icon again. When the menu opens, a check mark should appear before Set as Default.

Tip

Once you have set a printer as the default, you can still print from other installed printers. The Print dialog box offers you a selection each time you print, but the default printer will be the one that appears automatically.

74

Find a File on Your PC's Hard Drive

Use your computer's Find function when you have forgotten the name or location of a file. These instructions are for Windows 95/98/NT.

⊙ Steps

1 Click on the Start menu, then on Find, and then on Files or Folders.

2 Enter the filename in the box labelled Named. If you remember only key words or phrases used in the document, enter them in the box

Computers

labelled Containing Text. Try to choose a unique word or phrase to help narrow the search.

3   If you have an idea where the file is stored, use the Browse function to start the search in a particular folder.

4   Tick the box labelled Include Subfolders.

5   Click on Find Now. Within a few moments, you will receive a list of every file in the folder or drive that you selected whose name (or contents) includes the words you typed. (For example, if you entered "apples", you would get files called "Red apples" and "Golden delicious apples" in addition to "Apples".)

6   Double-click on the file to open it, or note the location so you can open the file later.

 Tips

Click on the Date tab to search for a file created or last used within a certain time frame.

Click on the Advanced tab to search for files created by a certain application.

You can also carry out file searches from within many software applications, such as Microsoft Word.

75

Find a File on a Mac

Mac OS 8.5 onwards (including OS X) features the powerful Sherlock search program.

Steps

1   For pre-System X Macs, click on the Apple menu and select Sherlock. OS X users can click on the Sherlock icon in the Dock. Alternatively – for both systems – from the Finder, press the keys Command-F.

2   Choose your search criteria. You can search by one or more attributes of the file (name, size, type, date modified, creator and so forth).

3   Choose a location to search. You can search locally or on a network.

4   To search the contents of a file for specific phrases, click on the Find by Content tab, then specify the phrase and a location in which to search. If the Find button is dimmed, click Index Volumes first.

5   Search the internet by keyword by selecting the Search internet tab.

6   Click Find to run the search.

Tips

When you search by name, the search finds all filenames that include the phrase you typed. So a search for "apple" would find files named "Aunt Mary's apple pie recipe" and "Apple Computer stock prices".

In the Sherlock results list, if you click once on the icon of a file, Sherlock will give its location, no matter how embedded within folders it may be. If you double-click on the icon, the application will launch.

76

Use Mac Files on a Windows Computer

If you save Mac files on a PC-formatted disk, you can open them on a PC, but you may lose some formatting. Here are tips for saving your Mac files so they transfer as well as possible.

◎Steps

1   If you can, save the file on your Mac using the same program (such as Microsoft Word or Excel, or WordPerfect) as you'll be using on the PC. Make sure to add the three-letter file extension (such as ".doc") when saving the file. You should then be able to open the file on a PC just by double-clicking it, and your formatting should be retained.

2   If you don't have the same program in Mac and PC versions, try saving your file in a common format, such as Rich Text Format (RTF), which most word processing software can read, or JPEG, if saving images. To open these, you might need to open the program you want on the PC, then use the Open command in the File menu.

3   If the first two options don't work, buy a conversion program for your PC to translate Mac file formats.

✳ Tip

You can save any text document as Plain Text; you'll lose all the
document's formatting, but the file will be guaranteed to open in any
word processing software.

77

Use Windows Files and Disks on a Mac

Any Macintosh built since the mid-1990s will be capable of
reading any removable media formatted for a PC. The
operating system contains translators that can open Windows
documents if you have the same application type on your
Mac.

⊙ Steps

1 Make sure Automatic Document Translation is turned on in the
Macintosh Easy Open or File Exchange control panel.

2 Put the PC disk in the Macintosh disk drive.

3 Double-click the PC disk icon.

4 Double-click the icon of the document you wish to open.

5 If the document doesn't open immediately, the Mac's Easy Open or
File Exchange control panel may give you a list of applications to try.
Choose the same type of application (graphics, word processing,
spreadsheet) as the document.

6 If this method doesn't work, open the Mac version of the PC
application that created the document. (For example, if it is a
Microsoft Word for Windows file, open Word on the Macintosh.) If you
lack that application, try a similar one (for example, the word
processor in AppleWorks). Open the File menu and choose Open,
then browse your disks for the PC file. If the file you are looking for
doesn't appear in the Open box, make sure that All Files is selected,
if possible, in the File Type menu. If that doesn't work, try another
program.

Computer Skills

✳ Tips

If your system software includes the PC Exchange control panel, make sure it is turned on.

If you can't open the file, or if its formatting is messed up, ask the person who created the document to save it again, this time in a translatable format, such as RTF (Rich Text Format).

Programs such as Word can also save files in the formats of earlier versions of the software.

⚠ Warning

You can't run or install Windows application programs on a Mac (unless, that is, you have installed Windows emulation software); you can only open documents.

78

Increase the Memory for a Macintosh Application

If you work with large documents, you may see a message complaining about insufficient memory (RAM). A document might not even open, or a program might run very slowly. You can assign more RAM to the application to see if that helps.

⊙ Steps

1 Single-click the icon for the application to which you want to allocate more memory. Be sure to exit the application first.

2 From the File menu choose Get Info, or press the keys Command-I.

3 In OS 8.5 and later versions, select Memory from the Show menu in the box that appears.

4 Type a new value into the Preferred Size box, perhaps 1.5 or 2 times the suggested size shown. You can decrease the memory in the same way.

5 Click the close box. Your change will take effect the next time you launch the application.

Computers

✳ Tip

If you attempt to increase the minimum size to a value larger than the preferred size, you will get an error message.

79

Format a PC Disk on a Mac

If you want to use Mac files on a PC, you need to make sure you use PC-formatted disks to transfer the files. (Macs read PC disks, but PCs don't read Mac disks.) But even if you have Mac disks, you can reformat them as PC disks using your Mac.

⊙ Steps

1 Insert a floppy disk (with write protection off) or Zip disk into its drive.

2 If a dialog box appears, telling you the disk is unreadable, you can format it by clicking on the appropriate button.

3 If a dialog box doesn't appear, select the disk by clicking on it, click on the Special menu option, and select Erase Disk.

4 Select the format you want from the menu in the dialog box that appears. Your Mac will format the disk and tell you when it's finished.

✳ Tip

Make sure there is nothing you want to keep on the disk before formatting it.

80

Protect a Computer From Viruses

If you think your computer may be infected, take all necessary steps to clear your system and avoid infecting other computers.

◎ Steps

1 Be cautious about what disks and files you accept from other people. Don't reuse disks that have been in other computers, don't download files from insecure sites, and don't open e-mail attachments unless you are expecting them. Be wary of messages and attachments, even from people you know, with vague subject lines and contents, such as "CHECK THIS" or "SEE THESE PICS!!!".

2 Obtain an anti-virus program to share disks more safely, download files from the internet and open e-mail attachments.

3 If your system gets a virus, visit your virus-scan software manufacturer's website and install any virus updates that are available. Then run the software. The software may not be able to delete the virus, but it may be able to identify it.

4 Search the web for information regarding your specific virus by typing the name of the virus or its associated file into a search engine, followed by the word "virus". For example, "Melissa virus", "BubbleBoy virus", and so on.

5 Download and install any software patches or other programs that will help you eliminate the virus. Or follow any instructions you find on deleting the virus manually.

6 Run another virus scan to make sure the virus was dealt with properly.

7 Employ extra caution when you receive attachments that end in the commonly used PC extensions .doc, .exe, .com, .xls or .ppt. Never open attachments that end in .vbs or .js, since a typical PC user would never have a reason to open such types of file.

✳ Tips

Keep up-to-date on virus alerts and install any patches released by software publishers.

If you think your computer has been infected with an e-mail virus that mails itself to people in your e-mail address book, phone those people and tell them not to open messages or attachments. Avoid sending out any messages until you have properly eliminated the virus.

Some viruses attach themselves to outgoing messages without your knowledge.

Generally, deleting the file that caused the virus isn't sufficient to eliminate the problem, since some viruses can create new files or corrupt existing files.

Computers

Choose a Good Computer Password

Whether it's for e-mail or for online banking, a good password should be easy to remember and difficult for others to work out.

⊙Steps

1 Use numbers as well as letters. If possible, use symbols such as % and *.

2 Randomly capitalize letters if the password is case-sensitive.

3 Use as many characters as possible – and a minimum of six.

4 Choose a string of characters that can be typed quickly without looking at the keyboard.

5 Avoid using your username, personal name, the personal names of friends or family members, your birthday or other things that people may know about you.

6 Avoid using an actual word from any language. If someone is serious about cracking your password, he or she will be able to run dictionaries from multiple languages against your account. However common, the word "password" is an obvious no-no.

7 Find an easy way to remember your password, but avoid writing it down.

8 Change your password every three to six months, especially if your account gives you access to restricted information.

9 If you have different accounts, it's wise to use a different password for each one, as long as you can remember them.

✱Tips

Acronyms for a phrase work well because they're much easier to remember – for example, "MNIJS" for "My name is John Smith.

For a more effective password, add a number or symbol at some point within the acronym. For example, "IMMNS?" for "Is my mother's name Susan?"

Computer Skills

Get Internet Access

The following steps describe how to access the internet using an internet service provider (ISP) and a computer modem. Many new computers include software that lets you set up an ISP account and connect to the internet immediately.

⊙ Steps

1 Buy a computer that has a modem or add a modem to your existing computer. Most internet service providers require at least an Intel 386 processor (or a Macintosh of any vintage) and a modem capable of at least 28.8 Kbps. New computers more than satisfy these requirements.

2 Make sure your modem is properly installed, and connect it to your nearest telephone socket.

3 Look on your computer's desktop for an icon that bears the name of an internet service provider. If you find one, double-click on the icon and follow instructions to install the software and activate your account.

4 If you can't find an icon and you are using Windows, open the Start menu and choose Settings, then Control Panel. In the window that appears, double-click the internet Options control panel. Click the Connections tab, then click the Setup button at the top of the window.

5 On a Mac, look for the Internet Setup Assistant in the Apple menu.

6 If your computer doesn't come with internet software, buy a computer or internet magazine and look for the names of ISPs in the back pages.

7 Look for special offers from large, commercial ISPs on television, in newspapers and in the mail.

8 Contact a provider and request installation software.

9 Once you've received the software, follow the installation instructions and set up your account.

✳ Tips

Fast access to the internet requires an ADSL "Broadband" connection.

Computers

Read your terms-of-service agreement carefully before signing on.

Consider rates and fees, e-mail and other features, technical support and system requirements when choosing an ISP.

Popular internet software can often be obtained free of charge on the "freebie" CD-ROMs that accompany computer and internet magazines.

83

Evaluate Free Internet Service Providers

Some ISPs don't charge for an account. Before you sign up, make sure that there are no hidden costs – either in terms of quality or cash.

◎ Steps

1 Find out what features the ISP offers. At a bare minimum, these should include e-mail and access to the World Wide Web. Other good features include access to newsgroups, instant messaging, chat and web hosting services.

2 Ask the same questions you would of other ISPs: What modem speeds does the ISP support? What operating systems? How many users per ISP modem? Is technical support available by phone?

3 Make sure the ISP is actually free. Read the fine print to see if there are any hidden charges that may show up later.

4 Determine how the company supports itself. Many free ISPs depend on advertising and end up bombarding customers with e-mail adverts.

5 Look for reviews to get a feel for user satisfaction and service.

6 Carefully review the ISP's terms of service and other fine print, keeping an eye out for any deceptive wording or other traps.

✱ Tip

There's nothing to lose if you sign up for a free ISP and end up not being satisfied – you haven't paid anything.

⚠ Warnings

Just because you don't have to pay a monthly fee, it might not be the cheapest way to connect to the internet. With all "free" ISP accounts you have to pay for your dial-up connection as if it were a telephone call. Most ISPs also offer "unmetered" access, meaning that for a monthly fee you have unlimited online access and your connection calls are not charged. This may provide huge savings in the long run.

84

Choose Broadband Internet Access

High-speed internet access is becoming more available. Depending on where you live, you may be able to get a Broadband (ADSL) connection.

⊙ Steps

1 Find out what services are available in your area. Although all Broadband lines are ultimately owned by British Telecom, BT is not the only provider. Contact your current ISP to see if it offers a Broadband upgrade, and also check computer periodicals and the web. If your local BT exchange is not equipped to provide Broadband services the only real option is a satellite installation. These are VERY expensive.

2 High-speed internet connections are also offered by most of the major cable companies.

3 Compare prices and speeds for various services.

4 Compare all hardware and installation costs.

5 After completing your basic research, decide whether the extra cost of increased speed is worth it. If you regularly send and receive large files or download MP3s or video clips from the internet, then a Broadband connection will make life a good deal easier. However, you may choose to wait until competition drives down prices.

6 However your connection is rated, expect actual ADSL speeds to vary according to your location, neighbourhood and usage at any given moment. You should be aware that your connection may not ever achieve the maximum speed advertised by the provider.

7 Before choosing your current telephone or cable company as your ISP, consider your level of satisfaction with its current service.

8 Find out how many other users will ultimately share access to your line – this will affect your connection speed.

Computers

9   Compare extras offered by high-speed ISPs, such as multiple
     accounts, domain aliasing and extra web space, if you'll use them.

Tips

Telephone and cable companies often provide free or subsidised
hardware and installation. A service-term contract is required with these
deals.

If Broadband is not available in your area you should register your
interest with the British Telecom website, bt.com. BT set targets for each
exchange; once that level is reached the exchange will be upgraded.

Regardless of whether you select your telephone company to be your
ISP, you will be dependent on it for ADSL service.

85

Avoid Giving Personal Information to Websites

Protect your privacy and security and minimise spam by using
caution when browsing the web.

⊙**Steps**

1   Do not give your credit card number to anyone online for any reason
     unless you are certain that the site is trustworthy and the browser
     connection is secure.

2   When shopping online, make sure the site is secure before providing
     your name and address.

3   Be selective when registering with websites. Take care that you read
     the company's privacy policy before providing personal information.
     Look for a little box somewhere in the registration form that allows the
     company to send you mail or – even worse – sell your personal
     information. This box is often pre-ticked. Remove the tick if you do
     not wish to receive mail from the site.

4   If you don't see any privacy information in the registration process,
     look for a statement somewhere on the site that describes the
     company's policy. If you don't find one, send e-mail to the site's
     webmaster. Ask that your information not be used.

World Wide Web

5   If you get e-mail from a site where you registered or shopped, and you didn't request it, look for a way to "unsubscribe" – this is usually described at the bottom of the e-mail message. If you don't find one, write back to the e-mail address and ask to be taken off the mailing list.

6   When posting to a web-based discussion board, use a false name. Avoid providing any contact information other than your e-mail address and the URL of your web page.

7   Try setting your browser to reject "cookies" – small files that load into your browser and enable a site to know that you've been there before. (Note: some site features won't work without cookies.)

✳ Tip

It's possible to configure most browsers only to accept cookies from specific websites.

86

Find Free Stuff on the Web

It's often said that nothing in life is free – but in many cases the internet may be an exception to this rule.

⊙ Steps

1   Enter whatever you're looking for, preceded by the word "free", into a web search engine. (If you're looking for free downloads in general, a good search string is "free stuff".)

2   Once you've found a site that offers what you're looking for, follow the instructions on how to download.

3   Check software manufacturers' websites for free trial versions of their software. Sometimes you can get a complete program to try; it will expire after a certain date. The trial program may have limited features.

4   Visit the websites for your favourite products to see if the sites give away free samples.

Computers

Tips

Some "free stuff" may have a catch: you might have to view ads while using a free ISP, for example. Always investigate first.

Free stuff includes screen savers, clip art, computer "wallpaper", and simple software.

⚠ **Warning**

Computer "shareware" can be downloaded for free, but you generally have to pay later on to keep using it.

87

Download Files

Downloading files may open up your hard disk to computer viruses. Avoid downloading from websites that you think might be dangerous or insecure.

◉ **Steps**

1   Visit the web page that has the link to the file you wish to download.

2   Click on the download link (usually a link that says "Download" or the name of the file).

3   Indicate which language and operating system you use, if necessary.

4   Select the download site nearest to you geographically, if given a choice. A window will pop up asking whether you wish to open the file or save it to disk.

5   Select "Save To Disk" to retain the file for future use. If you want to use it only once, select Open.

6   If you selected "Save To Disk", choose where you want the file to go on your hard disk. Most browsers then open a window indicating download progress – usually percentage downloaded and time remaining.

World Wide Web

88

Conduct an Advanced Internet Search

To conduct an advanced search on the internet, use Boolean operators, such as "AND" and "OR", to make your search as specific as possible.

⊙ Steps

1 Go to a web search engine.

2 To find documents containing an exact phrase, type the complete phrase, surrounded by quotation marks, into the search field. If, for example, you type in "fish sticks" (with the quotation marks) you will get a list of documents that contain the phrase "fish sticks", but NOT web pages that contain only the words "fish" or "sticks".

3 To find documents containing a pair of words, but not necessarily together, type those words separated by the word "AND" in capital letters. For example, typing "fish AND sticks" (without the quotation marks) will return web pages that contain "fish", "sticks" and "fish sticks".

4 To find documents containing either one word or the other, type those words separated by the word "OR" in capital letters. For example, typing "fish OR sticks" (without the quotation marks) will return documents that contain "fish" or "sticks", or both.

5 To exclude a word from your search, type the word you wish to exclude into the search field, preceded by the word "NOT" in capital letters. For example, typing "fish NOT salmon" (without the quotation

Computers

marks) will return only documents that contain the word "fish" but DON'T contain the word "salmon".

6   To find documents that contain two words separated by 10 to 25 words, type the two words separated by the word "NEAR" in capital letters, into the search field.

7   If your search expression is lengthy or complicated, use round brackets to separate the different parts. For example, typing "fish OR sticks NOT (salmon OR trout)" will generate entries that have the words "fish" or "sticks" or both, but do not have the words "salmon" or "trout".

✳ Tips

Check the directions for the search engine you're using. Some require very specific syntax.

Some search engines allow the following symbolic substitutions for Boolean words: & for AND, | for OR, ! for NOT, and ~ for NEAR. (Not all searches allow this, so if your query comes up blank, try using the words instead.)

Some search engines will not support the Boolean words "NEAR" or "NOT".

89

Shop Online

You can now buy just about anything online. If you haven't yet tried e-shopping, here's a general outline.

 Steps

1   If you don't know specifically which site to visit, use a search engine to find the product you're seeking. Or try a product-comparison site to check different prices or product reviews.

2   Visit several sites to find the best products and prices.

3   Most sites use a "shopping cart" system. As you browse the site and find items you want, click Add to Cart (or a similar button).

4   Specify a quantity and other relevant specifics (colour, size and so on) when you add an item to your shopping cart.

5   Click Continue Shopping (or a similar button) to keep browsing.
    Otherwise, click Proceed to Checkout (or something similar) to finalise
    your order.

6   For any kind of shopping site, provide your name, address, e-mail
    address, phone number and payment information when prompted
    during checkout. Once you've entered this information, you should be
    presented with an order-confirmation page, including all your items,
    the total price, and the address and other information you've entered.

7   Make sure your order is accurate and then confirm it.

✳ Tips

Most traditional mail order catalogue retailers now have websites.

Only shop from sites that use a secure server. If you're uneasy about
providing your credit card details online, look for a contact number and
pay over the phone.

In most cases, the online store will send you an e-mail message to
confirm the details of your order. Many online stores send e-mail updates
if any problems occur with your order.

⚠ Warning

If you buy in Europe from sites based in the US you may well be charged
customs duty on receipt of the goods.

90

Use the Internet to Locate People

Put the internet to work to find your best friend from infant
school, a long-lost relative or the flat-mate who left without
paying the phone bill.

◎ Steps

1   The person you're looking for may have a personal home page.
    To find out, simply type the person's first and last names into a web
    search engine and view the results.

2   To find old school or university chums, try the Friends Reunited
    website – friendsreunited.co.uk. (This is especially good if you want to

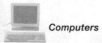

find out what old friends are up to without having to make direct contact!)

3   If the person you're looking for is a college student, he or she may have an e-mail account through the university's website.

4   The person may have an e-mail account through his or her job. If you know where the person works, visit the company's website and use its directory. If the site has no directory, try sending an e-mail message to the person at firstname.lastname@company.com.

5   If none of the above suggestions work, try an online directory website.

✳ Tip

Some online search services find e-mail addresses, some find phone numbers and postal addresses, and some find both.

91

Create Your First Website

These simple guidelines are for entry-level web programmers. Better options are available for more sophisticated users.

◉ Steps

Getting Started

1   Choose an ISP or other web hosting service to host your site.

2   Investigate several hosting services, considering maximum space, accessibility, reputation and terms of service.

3   Choose a suitable web-page editor. A number of simple editors are available for free download. This software lets you see what your site will look like as you build it, so you won't have to learn HTML or any other programming languages. Newer word processors, spreadsheets and other applications can also generate HTML files.

4   Your web-page editor will give you specific instructions about options such as naming your site, creating different sections, creating backgrounds, adding links and inserting images.

World Wide Web

Using Images

5 Create images for your site using a computer graphics program or by scanning photographs and other hard-copy images. You can also take photographs with a digital camera.

6 If you find an image on another web page that you'd like to use, send an e-mail to the page's owner or administrator and request permission to download and post it. Download an image from a website by right-clicking on it (or on a Mac, click and hold down the mouse) and select Save Picture.

Publishing Your Site

7 Your web host ISP may have its own system for uploading pages. Otherwise, obtain a File Transfer Protocol (FTP) program. Any will do.

8 Open your FTP program and log in to your host server by entering your login name and password.

9 Access the directory where your home page belongs. (Your web ISP will give you this information.) The directory address is usually in the form of /pub/username, /pub/www/username, or /pub/username/www. Your FTP program and host server will have specific instructions on how to access your directory.

10 Upload each page and graphic of your site according to the specific instructions of the FTP program and your host server.

✴ Tips

Many web hosts let you use your own "domain name" (such as me.com) if you have one, or will assign you a name.

Many graphics programs come with clip art – simple images in various categories – that you can use on your site.

Clip art CD-ROMs can be bought from software retailers.

You may want to limit the size of the images you include; larger images can make your page take a long time to load.

Your FTP program may give you a choice between ASCII and binary mode when uploading. Use ASCII mode for uploading pages, because pages are text files. Use binary mode for image files.

The steps shown are a general strategy for uploading your site. Your FTP program and web-page ISP will have more specific instructions.

Computers

⚠ Warning

To use content from another website, you need permission from the creator – unless it specifically states that text or images can be reused.

92

Choose a Domain Name for a Website

A domain name reflects your business or personal identity. Choose wisely.

⊙ Steps

1 Write down the name of your business. Remembering that short and sweet domain names are the easiest to remember, create a possible list using your business name (for example, smithauto.com, smauto.com, smitheys.com).

2 Create a list of services your business provides and a list of possible names from those services (for example, autorepair.com, fixcar.com, brokedown.com).

3 Use catchphrases from your brochure and other promotional materials to create additional possibilities.

4 For personal domain names, you could use your name, your pet's name, your hobbies, your surname or even your child's name.

5 Visit the Whois website (whois.org). Using Whois, you can type in your favourite names and see if they're already taken and by whom. If they are taken, keep trying with alternative choices.

6 If the popular ".com" name is taken, use other suffixes, such as ".co.uk", ".net" or ".org". Since users randomly searching for your site may be directed to the ".com" site first, ".net" and ".org" suffixes are best for personal rather than business domain names.

7 If you're really set on using a domain name that has already been taken, contact the owner of that domain name by checking the Administrative Contact section on the Whois site. Domain-name owners sometimes sell domain names they don't use.

World Wide Web

✳ Tip

Ask your family, friends and associates for their opinions of your choices.
What seems funny to you may be incomprehensible to someone else.

⚠ Warning

Don't use the name of a well-known company or product, or any
variation of that name, in the hope of attracting people to your site.
It may subject you to legal action.

93

Register a Domain Name

Setting up a website with your own domain name (me.com) is
a straightforward process, though finding a name you like
may prove difficult. Registration usually gives you exclusive
use of a domain name for a period of two years.

◎ Steps

1 Go to a website offering domain name registration, such as
   123-reg.co.uk.

2 Enter the name or phrase of the domain name you would like to
   register. Follow the rules regarding name length and format.

3 Search for the name.

4 If the name has already been registered, enter a new name and search
   again until you find one that is still available. If you first tried ".com" as
   a suffix, try ".co.uk", ".org" or ".net" instead.

5 Register the domain name.

6 Pay the filing fee online or through the mail, following the instructions
   on the website.

✳ Tips

Have a list of possible names ready when you visit the site.

The more unusual the name, the more likely it will be available. Most
common or well-known corporate names are taken.

Computers

If the domain name is already taken and you desperately want it, you may contact the owner and offer to buy it.

Once you have the domain name, contact your ISP to see about using it as your website or e-mail address.

94

Learn HTML

HTML, which stands for Hypertext Markup Language, is the formatting language used to create most web pages.

⊙ Steps

1. Call your local college or university. Many adult education centres also give courses on HTML and web design. Search the internet for online courses – many of which will be free of charge.

2. Purchase a book on HTML design. Book/CD-ROM combinations offer hands-on learning and web development tools.

3. Go to the HTML Writers Guild website (hwg.org) and sign up for the trial membership. The HTML Writers Guild offers classes in HTML, web design and web graphics for members.

4. Learn HTML on your own by looking at a page's source code. With your browser, open a simple, easy-to-read page. Open the View menu, then select Source or Page Source, depending on your browser. Study how the source code translates into the page you see in the browser.

5. Purchase an HTML reference manual to help you decipher the tags and their roles. You can even copy a page's source code and insert your own elements to see what happens.

6. Visit the World Wide Web Consortium at w3c.org to find an HTML tutorial and learn more about HTML's history.

7. Ask a web-page designer to teach you HTML as he or she designs a page for you. It costs a little more, but you will learn as you go and be able to update your own page.

✱ Tip

It is best to learn HTML before you use an HTML "assistant" or specific web design application. You can use HTML code to make changes that some programs won't allow you to make.

⚠ Warning

Use another's source code only to learn. Using parts of someone else's web page as your own is copyright infringement. Once you have learned HTML, you can then create your own pages.

95

Learn About Java

Java is a programming language created for the internet. You can use Java to create scripts, animated text and other visually interesting objects.

◎ Steps

1 Call your local college or university. Many adult education centres also give courses on Java and web design. Search the internet for online courses – many of which will be free of charge.

2 Log on to the website of Sun Microsystems, the company that created Java, to find tutorials and examples of Java programming.

3 Purchase a comprehensive book about Java. It should include an outline of Java history, an explanation of how the software works, examples and worksheets; some even come with interactive CD-ROMs.

4 Sign up for an online Java course. The HTML Writer's Guild (hwg.org) is one potential source.

5 Search the internet for some of the many useful user groups, forums and websites dedicated to Java.

6 Consider learning JavaScript, which is used in web browsers. Unrelated to Java, JavaScript is an "interpreted" language. JavaScript is easier to learn but more limited than Java.

Computers

7   If you're serious about programming, read up on general skills such as
     developing algorithms and designing data structures.

✳ Tips

Java applets are applications written in Java. They are typically attached
to web pages.

One of Java's strengths is that it is platform-independent. Java programs
can run on various operating systems, as long as the computer has a
Java virtual machine installed to interpret the Java code into commands
that will run on that system.

96

Publicise Your Website

Get the word out! Help people from all over the world find
your website.

◉ Steps

1   Register your site with your favourite internet search engines. Most
     search-engine sites have links (towards the bottom of the engine's
     home page) that say "Add a site" or "Add URL". Click on these links
     and follow the instructions.

2   Visit websites such as Submit It (submit-it.com), which help you
     submit your URL to multiple search engines simultaneously.

3   Visit sites that are related to or similar to your own, or maintained by
     your friends, and suggest linking to each other's pages.

4   Join a web ring, a group of websites on a particular topic that link to
     each other in a chain. Or start your own web ring. Visit the webring
     site (webring.org) for information.

5   Pay to place banner ads on well-trafficked websites; contact individual
     sites for their rates. Or join a free banner exchange, such as
     LinkExchange (linkexchange.com).

✳ Tip

Use META tags in your HTML pages to help your website come up in
more search-engine results. To learn more about META tags, visit web

developer sites, such as WebDeveloper.com or internetDay.com. For other tips about search-engine results, go to Search Engine Watch (searchenginewatch.com).

97

Get a Free E-mail Account

Free e-mail is typically web-based. It usually doesn't have as many features as internet service provider or work-based e-mail, but you can access it anywhere.

⊙ Steps

1   Decide what type of e-mail service would be best for you. Consider factors such as the volume of outgoing and incoming mail, message storing, the ability to send and receive attachments, frequency of use and security.

2   Do a search for "free e-mail" or "web mail" using a web search engine.

3   Visit various sites that offer free e-mail. Review their respective plans, features and terms of service.

4   Once you've found a free service that suits your e-mail needs, follow the site's instructions on how to set up your account.

✱ Tips

If you travel a lot or often use other people's computers, a web-based e-mail service will probably be best for you.

Some free e-mail services operate by inundating you with advertising e-mail messages from their sponsors; others make you view ads on the screen.

98

Send an E-mail Attachment

These instructions will give you the basics of how to send an e-mail attachment no matter which program you are using.

Computers

⊙ Steps

1 Go to your e-mail program.

2 Click the New Mail, Write Message or similar button, depending on your application, to create a new e-mail message.

3 Enter the address of the recipient in the To field.

4 Type a subject in the Subject field.

5 Add a message to the body of the e-mail as usual.

6 Click the Attachments button (many programs show this as a paperclip icon). Also look for an Insert File or Insert Attachment option in the File menu.

7 Browse your files to find the attachment you want to send. You may need to click on a Browse or Find button to see your directory.

8 Click on the filename. If your program allows you to attach more than one file at once, hold down the Control key (or Shift key on a Mac) as you select another one.

9 Click the Attach Insert or Open button, depending on your e-mail program.

10 To send another file located in a different area of the hard disk, click the Attachments button again and repeat the previous steps.

11 Click the Send button when you're done.

✱ Tips

Change picture attachments to the JPEG format. They'll take up less space and may be sent faster in that format.

Make sure the recipient can read your attachment. Most word processors can read RTF (Rich Text Format). Web browsers can invariably open JPEG and GIF image files.

If you're sending files to a person who uses a modem, be careful about sending large files (300K or more) – they can take a long time to download.

Consider compressing your files with a utility such as WinZip or StuffIt. Your recipient may need to have the same compression software as you, although some programs are able to create "self-extracting" files that decompress automatically.

E-Mail and Newsgroups

Create Your Own E-mail Mailing List

By creating your own e-mail mailing list, you can easily send copies of a single message to a group of recipients.

⊙ Steps

1   Collect the e-mail addresses of your recipients.

2   Open your e-mail program and save these names as a group. Look for a function that is called something like Address Book, Contacts or Nicknames. Name the group and enter your recipients' e-mail addresses separated by commas or semicolons. Click Save. Note that many e-mail programs require that you enter all of the individual addresses to your Address Book before you can add them to a group.

3   Open a new message and address it to yourself.

4   Add the subject and body of the message.

5   Put the group e-mail addresses in the field marked BCC (blind carbon copy). Your e-mail software should allow you to do this automatically from the Address Book or from the Nickname function. If it doesn't, copy the list and paste it in the BCC field of your message.

6   Click Send. The original message will be sent to you, as you entered your own address in the To field.

7   Each member of the group will receive a copy of the message.

✳ Tips

Using the BCC field instead of the CC field allows the messages to be sent without showing each recipient the e-mail addresses of the other recipients. However, not all e-mail programs support the BCC feature.

If you have a large mailing list (hundreds or thousands), you may want to consider buying specially designed bulk e-mail software. To avoid being accused of spamming, include only the addresses of people who have already agreed to receive your messages.

Stop Unwanted E-mail

As anyone who's ever had an inbox cluttered with unwanted advertisements knows, spam, or unsolicited commercial e-mail, can be a big problem.

⊙ Steps

1 Contact your ISP and complain. ISPs don't like spam any more than you do; the mail clogs their servers. The ISP may be able to filter out mail from a suspected spammer address.

2 Avoid displaying your e-mail address in internet chat rooms and only give out your e-mail address on secure sites.

3 Avoid including your e-mail address when you post to newsgroups.

4 Send a complaint message to the postmaster at the spammer's ISP, if you can figure it out. Many spammers forge return addresses, but you can sometimes figure out the ISP from the full e-mail header. In some e-mail programs you can right-click on the e-mail message and choose Options or Properties to see this information.

5 Be careful when selecting a free ISP or e-mail account. Some of these services make their money by letting "sponsors" send e-mail messages to their subscribers.

6 If your e-mail provider doesn't have a built-in spam filter, search the web for e-mail filters and other anti-spam software. Many of these programs are free and can be easily installed.

✱ Tip

To reduce spam in your e-mail account, open a second, free e-mail account which you use exclusively for web registrations, chat rooms and mailing lists (see 97 "Get a Free E-mail Account").

⚠ Warning

Don't reply to spam unless the message includes specific instructions for removing yourself from a mailing list. In most cases, responding only verifies that your e-mail address is active. Sometimes the spammer will have forged a return address, so by responding you're actually bothering an innocent person.

E-Mail and Newsgroups

Read a Newsgroup on the Internet

Internet newsgroups are a great way to share information online. Once you have a newsreader set up on your computer, reading and posting to newsgroups is relatively simple.

◎ Steps

1 Get your news server name from your ISP or network administrator.

2 Determine whether your current ISP software, e-mail program or web browser includes a newsreader – most of them do. If not, download and install one.

3 Configure your newsreader by inputting your news server address and any other information it requests (it might ask for an e-mail address and mail server as well).

4 Use your reader to call up a list of available newsgroups. This list will probably pop up during setup the first time you use your reader.

5 Look through the hierarchical list of newsgroups to find any that sound interesting. Let the prefixes of each group (such as "comp" for computer-related topics and "rec" for recreational topics) guide your search. The other words in the name go from general to more specific keywords.

6 Subscribe to whichever newsgroups you want to read or post to. (Note that some readers allow you to read newsgroup messages without your having to subscribe.)

7 Select the newsgroup you want to read.

8 Select a message by double-clicking on the subject. (Note that different readers may have different ways of reading messages.)

✱ Tips

Your ISP may not subscribe to all your chosen newsgroups. If possible, use a separate reader to maximise your access to the internet. Newsgroups that begin with "alt" (denoting "alternative" topics) may be especially hard to find on some ISPs.

If you come across a newsgroup message that appears to be gibberish, it may be a message encrypted into "Rot13". This is a simple encryption

code that replaces each letter with the letter that is 13 spots ahead of it in the alphabet. This coding is used mainly to protect people from possibly offensive postings. You can decode these messages by hand, or your reader may have a Rot13 decoding utility.

102

Use Online Forums

Online forums – also called discussion boards – function in a similar way to newsgroups, except that they are available through ISPs and individual websites.

◎ Steps

1 Explore some of the forums and special-interest groups on your ISP or online service.

2 Use a search engine and look for websites that focus on your interests. Many of these will have forums or chats.

3 Begin by reading the "posts" (messages) and follow the current "threads" (comments related to a single topic) for several days. See if the group has a FAQ (frequently asked questions) document.

4 Write a post of your own. Be prepared for a mixed response.

5 Explain yourself if someone takes exception to your comments, but do not get into a heated argument via posts.

6 Determine whether your forum companions get together for online chat sessions. Join in if they do.

7 Send e-mail to your new friends and develop new relationships.

✳ Tips

Keep your initial posts short and noncontroversial.

Befriend a veteran or two and ask about the group's taboos.

Represent yourself accurately; you may want to meet the forum regulars one day.

103

Buy a Fax Machine

When looking for a fax machine, consider quality, price and special features. If you need to send faxes but not receive them, consider a computer-based fax modem as an alternative.

⊙ Steps

1 Determine the type of machine you want. Choose a film-cartridge fax machine for adequate print quality; look for an ink-jet fax machine to achieve better print quality at a slightly higher price; if you can afford to pay more, buy a laser fax machine for the best print quality – if you receive a lot of faxes, the higher purchase price will quickly be offset by the low cost of use.

2 Look for machines with four choices for image quality.

3 Make sure the machine can print 64 shades of grey if you'll be receiving and copying both text and images. Colour-capable machines are also available, but they're expensive.

4 Consider how many – if any – speed-dial numbers you'll need.

5 Decide whether you need an integrated digital answering machine.

6 Compare each model's capacity for feeding multiple pages, storing received faxes when the machine is out of paper and "broadcast" faxing to a group of recipients.

7 Evaluate how easy the machine is to use.

8 Look for advanced business features, if necessary, such as delayed transmission, the ability to "poll" other fax machines, copy reduction and enlargement, and "shrink to fit" A4 pages.

9   Budget for everything you'll need, such as paper, extra cartridges, a mains surge suppressor and a service contract.

10 Consider the service contracts offered by the dealer. Do they include maintenance and cover normal wear?

11 Base your final decision on functionality and initial and ongoing costs.

✱ Tips

You don't need to get a separate phone line (the fax or an attached answering machine may be able to tell incoming faxes from voice calls, or the sender can input a fax-activation code), but an extra line is convenient if you're doing a lot of faxing.

Be sure to budget for such consumable items as paper and cartridges or ink.

A typical film cartridge produces around 350 pages. To calculate the cost per page, divide the price of the cartridge by the number of pages.

Toner cartridges for laser fax machines may produce up to several thousand pages, making them cheaper to run than ink-jet or film faxes; the basic cost of the unit may be considerably greater, though.

104

Choose a Mobile Phone

Can't bear to be out of contact with the rest of the world for a single second? Then get yourself a mobile phone.

⊙ Steps

1   Estimate how many calls per week you'll make on your mobile and how many minutes you'll spend talking.

2   Determine how much you're willing to pay for your mobile phone and for the monthly service.

3   Decide which features are important to you: size and weight, colour options, number storage, messaging, customised settings, fax, web capabilities, and caller identification to display the phone number (or name, if programmed) of an incoming call. Some of the new generation of mobile phones can even take photographs and send

Telecommunications

them to other suitably equipped phones, or download and play MP3 tunes.

4 Take accessories into account: You'll need an AC adaptor for charging the phone, and you might also want a car adaptor, a carrying case or fun goodies such as removable coloured faceplates ("fascias").

5 Consult consumer reports in magazines, newspapers, the web and other news media for opinions on different phones and providers.

6 Decide on a service provider in concert with your choice of phone (see the next eHow), since certain plans require the use of specific phones.

✳ Tip

Service providers sometimes offer deals including free phones or great discounts when you sign up for their plans. Look around for those.

⚠ Warning

Review the terms of the contract to ensure that there are no early-cancellation fees.

105

Choose a Mobile Phone Service Provider

Estimate your calling needs before you start investigating plans, and then find one that most closely matches how you think you'll use your mobile phone.

◉ Steps

1 Estimate how much you're willing to pay, and whether to go for a pay-as-you-go plan or one that gives a set amount of "free" time for a monthly fee.

2 Decide what geographic coverage you need. Will you mostly be using your phone locally or will you also use it travelling overseas ("roaming")?

3 See what ALL of the mobile phone providers have to offer before taking the plunge. Since the UK has a very small number of players in this field, this kind of research can best be done in specialised mobile

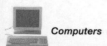

phone shops. Review the pricing plans, paying particular attention to charges for "roaming" (use outside the provider's area of coverage), texting, and making calls during peak hours.

✱ Tip

Subscribers who pay a higher fixed monthly fee for a greater amount of "free" talk time are rewarded with cheaper calls above their monthly limit.

⚠ Warning

Review the terms of the contract to ensure that there are no early-cancellation fees.

106

Select a Pager Service

A wide assortment of pager services is available. Be careful not to pay for features you don't want.

◎ Steps

1 Decide where and when you want your pager to work. Pager services now offer plans that can cover you nationwide or even worldwide.

2 Decide if you need to purchase a pager or just hire one temporarily – for an important business event, or the birth of a child, for example.

3 Determine whether you want the capability to send messages from your pager.

4 Decide if you want callers to be able to leave a voice message or just a phone number. Voice mail can prove convenient if you are out of range of the pager or you have turned the pager off when a call comes in.

5 Contact the major pager service providers – all of them should have dedicated websites.

6 Find out if the pager service offers customer service 24 hours a day, seven days a week.

7 Investigate whether it offers a live operator who can take messages.

Telecommunications

8   Determine if each plan the service offers is flexible. Make certain that there is a means for you to get undelivered or stored messages when your pager is within the service area.

9   Find out if the pager service offers hardware – that is, a pager unit – that enables you to access all of the features in your chosen plan.

 Tip

Yearly plans are charged at a less expensive rate than month-to-month plans.

107

Synchronise Your Palm Device With Your Computer

One of the greatest strengths of the palm computing platform is the ability to add information on either a computer or palm-held device, then synchronise the information between the two. (This eHow assumes that the Palm desktop has already been installed successfully on your computer.)

◎ **Steps**

1   Be sure HotSync Manager is running.

2   On a Macintosh, launch HotSync Manager from the Instant Palm Desktop and make certain HotSync is enabled.

3   In Windows, check to see that the HotSync icon appears in the Windows task bar.

4   Place the palm device in the cradle. Then press the HotSync button on the cradle.

5   If nothing happens, tap the HotSync icon on the palm screen, then tap Local Sync.

6   Wait for the synchronisation to be complete, then launch Palm Desktop. You'll notice that items added to the palm device now appear on the Palm Desktop, and items added to the Palm Desktop now appear on the palm device.

Tips

If you're having trouble performing a HotSync operation, try lowering the connection speed.

If you want to use a HotSync cable instead of a cradle, you must initiate the HotSync from the Palm device.

You can synchronize multiple Palm devices with one PC. You'll be prompted to select a user the first time you perform a HotSync.

"Beam" a File to Another Palm Device

One of the high cool factors in using a palm-held device is the capability to "beam" information wirelessly from one device to another. To beam and receive beams, you must be using at least a Palm III, or an earlier device upgraded to a Palm III.

⊚ **Steps**

Beam an Application Entry (Data)

1   Place the two palm devices facing each other, no more than a metre apart.

2   Select the file you want to beam.

3   Tap the menu icon, and then display the Record drop-down menu.

4   Choose Beam Memo if you are using the Memo Pad.

5   Choose Beam Event if you are using the Date Book.

6   Choose Beam Address if you are using the Address List. You must have a specific address entry selected to beam an address.

7   Choose Beam Item if you are using the To Do List.

Beam an Application Program

1   Place the two palm devices facing each other, no more than a metre apart.

2   Tap the Applications icon (Palm III) or the House icon (above Palm III) to display the Applications list.

3 Tap the Menu icon, then choose Beam from the App drop-down menu.

4 Select an application from the Beam box, and then tap Beam.

5 Applications with a padlock symbol next to the size of the application are locked and cannot be beamed.

6 Tap Done to close the Beam box.

 Tips

It can be useful to beam an application entry – such as directions to a restaurant – from one device to another. It can also be fun to beam shareware games to all your friends.

You can beam entire categories of information from the Address Book, To Do list and Memo Pad.

If you are finding it difficult to beam, try placing both palm devices on a flat surface.

109

Brew a Pot of Tea

When you're feeling parched, there's nothing more refreshing than a cup of tea that has been properly brewed in the traditional way in a teapot.

◉ **Steps**

1 Fill a kettle with fresh, cold water, adding enough to make the desired amount of tea, plus some extra to allow for evaporation and to pre-warm the teapot.

2 Wait until the water is near boiling, then pour a little into the teapot and swirl it around. This warms the pot so that it is at an optimum temperature for holding the tea. Empty the pot.

3 For each cup of tea, place 1 rounded teaspoon of leaves into the warmed pot. (If your pot has a strainer basket, use that.)

4 Allow the water to come to the boil.

5 Pour the water from the kettle over the leaves in the teapot.

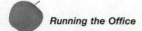

Running the Office

6   Let the tea steep for 3 to 5 minutes, depending on the size of the leaves. Allow a longer steeping time for larger leaves.

7   Stir just before serving, then pour the tea through a strainer into the cups. You might add sugar, milk, honey or lemon (or a combination, but don't use lemon and milk together).

8   Keep the pot covered with a tea cosy to keep the tea warm, and enjoy.

✴ Tips

If you do not want to use a strainer, place the tea leaves in a tea infuser, filter or mesh tea ball instead. You can also purchase tea pots with removable infusion baskets. You can use tea bags in a teapot, but the quality of tea in bags is never as good as that of loose tea.

Transfer steeped tea into another heated teapot to avoid the bitter taste that can result from its sitting on the leaves for a long period of time.

110

Brew a Pot of Coffee

Filter coffee can be made in a coffee percolator or simply by placing a filter holder over a pot or cup.

⊙ Steps

Using a Filter Coffeemaker

1   Fill the coffeemaker's jug with fresh, cold water.

2   Place 2 tbsp coffee in the filter for every 175 ml (6 fl oz) of water. (Sometimes the cups marked are more than 175 ml (6 fl oz), so check the instructions.)

3   Pour the water into the reservoir and replace the jug.

4   Turn on the percolator.

Using a Filter Holder (Manual Method)

1   Boil water, then let it rest briefly to achieve the optimum brewing temperature of 90–96 °C (195–205 °F).

2   Place a filter holder over a coffeepot or cup.

3   Place a filter in the holder.

4   Add about 2 level tbsp ground coffee to the filter holder per 175 ml (6 fl oz) of water, or adjust if you like it weaker or stronger.

5   Pour about 3 tbsp of water over the grounds to wet them.

6   Wait a few seconds for the grounds to expand.

7   Pour the rest of the water over the grounds. Let it drip through the grounds, but be sure to remove the grounds before the last of the water has drained into the pot or cup. Coffee grounds can overextract and get a bitter taste.

Using a Cafetière

1   Remove the lid and plunger from the cafetière.

2   Fill a kettle with fresh, cold water, adding enough to make the desired amount of coffee (175 ml (6 fl oz) per cup), plus some extra to allow for evaporation and to pre-warm the cafetière.

3   Wait until the water is near boiling, then pour a little into the cafetière and swirl it around to warm the jug. Empty the jug.

4   Place about 2 level tbsp ground coffee in the jug for each cup required.

5   Allow the water in the kettle to boil, then let it rest briefly to achieve the optimum brewing temperature of 90-96°C (195-205°F).

6   Pour the required amount of water onto the coffee.

7   Allow the coffee to steep for a few minutes.

8   Place the plunger and lid on the jug and very carefully press the plunger down to the bottom of the jug, to trap the ground coffee at the bottom of the jug.

✱ Tip

Keep coffee warm on a ring or hot plate for no more than 20 minutes. After 20 minutes, coffee takes on a "stewed", bitter taste. Reheating coffee increases its bitterness and is not recommended.

Clean a Coffeemaker

One way to make your coffee taste better is to keep your coffeemaker clean and free of hard-water deposits.

⊙Steps

1   Put the filter basket in place.

2   Combine one part white vinegar with one part water in the pot; pour it into the reservoir and replace the pot. Turn the machine on.

3   Allow the solution to empty completely into the pot.

4   Turn the coffeemaker off and rinse the pot and filter basket with warm water.

5   Pour clean water into the coffeemaker, replace the pot and turn the machine on.

6   Allow the water to empty completely into the pot.

7   Rinse the pot.

8   Wipe the outside of the coffeemaker with a soapy sponge and polish It dry.

✱Tips

Clean your coffeemaker weekly if you make a lot of coffee.

Consider purchasing a special coffeemaker cleaner. Follow the manufacturer's directions.

Rinse the pot and basket every day with warm water and once a week with mild soap and warm water.

Things You'll Need

☐ white vinegar

☐ sponge

Clean a Fridge

Is there anything more unpleasant than opening a fridge door only to be greeted by some unexpected foul odour? It must be time to give your fridge a good going over.

⊙ Steps

1 Turn the temperature-control knob inside the fridge to "Off". If you have a fridge with a drip pan underneath, remove it to clean.

2 Take everything out of the fridge.

3 Throw away any food that is mouldy, out of date or otherwise spoiled.

4 Take all removable parts out of the fridge, including shelves, wire racks and drawers.

5 Fill the sink with warm, soapy water (use a mild washing-up liquid).

6 Wipe any food matter out of the drawers.

7 Hand-wash the shelves, wire racks and drawers, then rinse them in warm water.

8 Let the shelves, wire racks and drawers drain in a dish rack, on paper towels or on newspapers.

9 Remove any food matter from the bottom of the fridge.

10 Wash the inside of the fridge using a sponge or dishcloth and the warm, soapy water. Remember the compartments and door racks.

11 Rinse the inside of the fridge with a sponge or dishcloth and clean warm water.

12 For odour control, use a solution of baking soda and warm water to wash the inside of the fridge (a solution of a few drops of vinegar in a bowl of warm water is also effective); apply and rinse. Leave a box of bicarbonate of soda in the fridge to keep odours to a minimum.

13 Replace all shelves, wire racks and drawers.

14 Wash the outside of the fridge and the door seal – the rubber moulding around the door – with warm, soapy water; rinse and wipe dry.

15 Turn the temperature control knob inside the fridge back to the recommended setting.

16 Return the food to the fridge, first wiping off any bottles or jars that
are sticky.

✳ Tip

**Condenser coils should be vacuumed several times a year to prevent
dust build-up.**

⚠ Warning

Never use harsh cleaners or scouring pads in or on the fridge.

Things You'll Need

☐ mild washing-up liquid

☐ sponge or dishcloths

☐ bicarbonate of soda or vinegar

113

Clean a Toilet

**This will probably never be your favourite chore, but it is one
of the most important.**

◎ Steps

1 Open the toilet windows and door, or turn on the fan. You need good
ventilation when working with household cleaners.

2 Put on rubber gloves and lift the toilet seat. Flush the toilet to wet the
sides of the bowl.

3 Apply a generous amount of powder or liquid toilet cleaner to the
bowl, focusing on getting it along the sides and under the rim, not just
in the water. Be sure to follow the directions for your type of toilet
bowl cleaner.

4 Let the cleaner stand for the recommended length of time.

5 Using the toilet brush, swab all around the interior of the bowl, paying
special attention to the area immediately beneath the rim, and to the
water line.

6 Flush the toilet to rinse. As the water in the bowl is replaced,
thoroughly rinse the toilet brush in the incoming water.

Housekeeping

7   Notice if the toilet bowl has developed a ring. If it has, scrub the stain with a wet pumice stone. Be sure the pumice remains wet throughout the process.

8   Spray the seat, the underside of the seat and the rim with disinfectant.

9   Wipe down the base, lid and tank top with disinfectant.

10 Allow the disinfectant to dry before using the toilet.

✳ Tip

High-pressure steam cleaners are very effective for cleaning toilets.

⚠ Warning

Never mix cleaners. The fumes could be deadly.

Things You'll Need

☐ rubber gloves

☐ toilet cleaner

☐ toilet brush

☐ pumice stone

☐ disinfectant

Running the Office

Many local authorities have recycling schemes that pick up tins, bottles and newspapers. Some may also collect motor oil and other hazardous waste. But did you know that still other common materials can be safely recycled? Here's how to help find a few of these items a happy second home.

Printer and photocopier cartridges

- Before you throw a cartridge away, be aware that printer cartridges can be recycled up to six times without any loss of quality.

- Read the manufacturer's instructions on the cartridge packing. It may tell you how to send back the cartridge free of charge so it can be refilled.

- You can find further information on dealing with used printer cartridges in the UK on the web pages of Eurosource (esel.co.uk) and the Cartridge Recycling Scheme (cartridge-recycling.org.uk) .

- Look at empty-inkjet-cartridges.com to find out how you can sell used printer cartridges.

Computer Equipment

- Write down all the information about the old computer, such as its brand, type and model number, and which peripherals you wish to recycle.

- If you intend to continue using software currently loaded on an old machine, to avoid infringing copyright laws you should erase the contents of hard drives to be discarded. Obviously you should delete any personal files.

- Contact local schools or charities that might be able to make use of your equipment.

- Look at the web pages of Computer Aid (computer-aid.org) or UK Computer Recycling (uk-cr.org.uk) for more details on recycling computer technology in Great Britain.

reference

Housekeeping

Packing "peanuts"

(These are the small "S-shaped" foam blocks used to protect items packed in boxes during transit.)

- Determine whether the peanuts are made from a vegetable derivative by running water on a few. If they disintegrate, they will decompose. Put them in a compost bin.

- Check with your local council to see if it will pick up large quantities of packing peanuts.

- Look under packaging or shipping in the Yellow Pages for a store that will accept the peanuts – some may let you drop them off.

Batteries and Mobile Phones

- Take old car batteries to your local garage, or auto parts store.

- Many recycling centres will dispose of old car batteries.

- You can take unwanted mobile phones into any branch of Oxfam for recycling.

- Phone manufacturers such as Nokia will accept old phones. Look at their web pages (nokia.com).

- Look out for special trade-in offers where your mobile phone service provider may offer you a part-exchange deal on a new and better phone.

- FoneBak is a government-supported scheme for the recycling of mobile phones (fonebak.co.uk).

Clean Out a Cupboard

Are the contents of your cupboards a mystery? Set aside a couple of hours to clean them out. All it takes is a little organisation to bring order to the chaos.

⊙ Steps

1   Start with a clean room, or you'll make an even bigger – not to mention more intimidating – mess as you clean out the cupboards.

2   Choose one area of the cupboard to focus on, such as a shelf, and begin there. It will make the overall task seem less daunting if you break it up into manageable parts.

3   Get three boxes and mark them "Rubbish", "Out of Place" and "Charity".

4   Evaluate each item you remove from the cupboard. Ask yourself if you have used the item in the past 12 months. If not, it's time to think seriously about getting rid of it.

5   Put things for charity shops in the "Charity" box.

6   Stash things that belong in other departments in the "Out of Place box". (Give these things the 12-month test, too.)

7   Put as much as possible into the Rubbish box. You'll be surprised at how cathartic this can be!

8   Sort the items you wish to keep into categories. Clearly label them and return them to the cupboard.

✽ Tips

Give yourself a time limit. If you plan to devote 1½ hours to cleaning, don't do more than that. It will still be there later.

Some charities will come to to pick up unused items.

⚠ Warning

Get permission to throw away things that do not belong to you personally.

116

Clean Painted Walls

They may be vertical surfaces, but even your walls get dirty.
When you get the notion, get your wall cleaning in motion.

⊙ Steps

1 Protect your floors with newspapers or towels.

2 Brush cobwebs and dust from the wall with a soft-bristled brush.

3 Remove any remaining dirt with a dry sponge. Rub it along the wall to
   lift away dirt.

4 Fill a bucket about three-quarters full with warm water.

5 Add a small amount of washing-up liquid – about as much as it takes
   to clean a sink full of dishes – to the bucket. This is the cleaning
   bucket.

6 Place a second, empty bucket near the cleaning bucket. (You'll use
   this when you wring out the cleaning sponge.)

7 Dip a small portion of the flat face of a sponge into the cleaning
   bucket until it is damp.

8 Spread the cleaning solution on the wall with the sponge, beginning at
   the top and working towards the bottom. Use a ladder to reach the
   high spots on the wall.

9 Squeeze – but do not wring out – the sponge over the empty bucket
   after wetting the entire surface of the wall.

10 Blot the surface of the wall you've just cleaned with the sponge to lift
   any further dirt from its surface.

11 Repeat this process until you have covered the wall.

12 Dry the wall using a clean towel.

Commercial products are widely available to remove oil-based or grease stains.

Things You'll Need

- ☐ newspapers or towels
- ☐ soft-bristled brush
- ☐ dry sponge
- ☐ buckets
- ☐ washing-up liquid
- ☐ sponge
- ☐ ladder
- ☐ clean towel

117

Clean a Polyurethane-Coated Hardwood Floor

Polyurethane-finished hardwood floors are tough and will last for years with the proper care. Fortunately, caring for these floors is very straightforward.

Steps

1 Clear the room of rugs and as much furniture as possible. This helps to ensure that the entire floor gets equal treatment.

2 Sweep and/or vacuum the floor carefully. Dirt left on the floor during mopping can act as an abrasive.

3 Mix about 1 tsp of washing-up liquid into a large bucket full of warm water. The exact mixture isn't crucial; just keep the amount of detergent to a bare minimum.

4 Start mopping in a corner along the wall farthest from the door, and mop the entire floor with firm strokes. Make sure the mop is well wrung out and not dripping. Both foam and string mop heads will work.

5 Use new solution when the water begins to grow cloudy or dirty.

6 Repeat the process with fresh water (not soapy) once the entire surface has been thoroughly mopped with the cleaning solution. This will pick up the soapy residue and leave your floor clean and shiny.

7 Polish dry with clean, dry towels.

⚠ Warnings

Be careful with water; you may need to spot-clean around any unsealed gaps between the boards. Always polish the floor dry.

Never use cleaning oils or furniture polishes on polyurethane-coated floors – these can leave a residue that will cause refinishing problems later. Certain chemical-based strippers can damage the finish as well.

Things You'll Need

☐ washing-up liquid

☐ bucket

☐ mop

☐ towels

118

Deep-Clean Your Carpet

For heavily soiled carpets, shampooing is recommended, rather than spot-cleaning. Wet-cleaner machines spray and remove hot detergent solution while cleaning the carpet.

⊙ Steps

1 Purchase or hire a wet-cleaner machine, also known as a steamer, at a hardware or DIY shop. When you rent a machine, the necessary cleaning products are usually included or can be purchased at the hire shop.

2 Vacuum the floor thoroughly.

3 Spray heavily soiled areas with pre-spray or traffic-lane cleaner. For those really dirty areas, increase the amount of pre-spray used instead of increasing the amount of carpet shampoo.

4 Fill the machine's hose or reservoir with hot tap water.

5 Use the machine and carpet shampoo according to the steamer manufacturer's instructions.

6 Maximise the amount of water removed from the carpet by making a water-extraction pass with the water spray on, and then again with the spray off. Test the carpet with your hand. If your hand comes away with water droplets, extract again with the spray off; if your hand comes away damp and the carpet feels wrung out, you have extracted correctly.

7 Wait overnight for the carpet to dry before walking on it. To help it dry thoroughly, open windows and use fans.

Tips

Special solutions are available to treat pet stains and odours.

To help your cleaning last longer, neutralise detergent residue left on the carpet by steaming with a rinse made up of a few drops of vinegar in a bowl of water.

⚠ Warning

Over-saturating the carpet can cause water to soak through and damage the floor underneath.

Things You'll Need

☐ wet-cleaner machine (steamer)

☐ pre-spray or traffic-lane cleaner

☐ carpet shampoo

119

Clean Vinyl and Plastic Blinds

Don't go blindly into cleaning your window dressings. Follow these easy steps.

◎ Steps

Cleaning Monthly

1 Lower the blinds and close the slats.

2   Wipe with a damp rag. Avoid applying too much pressure to the blinds when scrubbing, as most are prone to denting and bending.

3   Close the slats in the opposite direction and wipe the other side.

Cleaning Deeply

1   Remove the blinds from the window.

2   Release the blinds completely and lay them outside, on a dust sheet.

3   Spray the blinds with an all-purpose cleaner. Allow the cleaner to sit for a few minutes.

4   Scrub the blinds gently with a soft-bristled brush in a motion parallel to the slats.

5   Turn the blinds over and repeat this process.

6   Hang or hold up the blinds and rinse with a hose.

7   Shake as much moisture from the blinds as possible.

8   Hang the blinds outside and allow them to dry.

Tips

Cloth blinds should be vacuumed regularly and professionally cleaned every two years.

Most blinds can be professionally cleaned.

Things You'll Need

☐ damp rag

☐ dust sheet

☐ all-purpose cleaner

☐ soft-bristled brush

☐ hose

120
Clean Windows

Brighten up your outlook by stripping off those layers of grime. Here's how to get your windows squeaky clean and streak free.

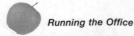

Running the Office

⊙ Steps

1 Prepare a cleaning solution of either four to six drops of washing-up liquid or the recommended amount of a proprietory window-cleaning product in a bowl of water. (Alternatively use a window-cleaning spray and follow the instructions on the package.)

2 Dip a sponge into the solution, allowing the sponge to absorb just enough water to cover the window without flooding it.

3 Wash the surface of the window with the sponge, paying attention to the sides and corners of the window frame, where dirt and grime tend to build up.

4 Dip a squeegee into a bucket of clean water.

5 Press the squeegee lightly into the surface of the window, starting at the top and pulling down vertically, stopping a few inches before the bottom of the window.

6 Wipe off the squeegee with a paper towel.

7 Press the squeegee down the area of the window directly beside the one you just cleaned, stopping at the same place.

8 Wipe off the squeegee with a paper towel.

9 Continue this process until the entire surface of the window except the final few inches at the bottom has been cleaned.

10 Pull the squeegee horizontally across the bottom section of the window and wipe the squeegee off with a paper towel.

11 Wipe off the water at the bottom of the window frame – where a great deal of moisture has by now collected – with a paper towel.

✱ Tip

For hard-to-reach windows, you can buy squeegee extension poles, specifically made for washing windows.

Things You'll Need

☐ window-cleaning product

☐ washing-up liquid

☐ sponge

☐ squeegee

☐ bucket

☐ paper towels

Clean Wood Walls and Panelling

Some people hesitate to clean wood panelling for fear of damage. Here's how to clean those walls and panels safely.

◎Steps

1 Dust wood walls and panelling with a soft rag, or vacuum with a vacuum cleaner brush about every two weeks.

2 Use a soft cloth to apply wood cleaner to particularly dirty wood according to the manufacturer's directions.

3 For tough stains, clean the wood with white spirit as a last resort. To test for staining, use a soft cloth to apply the spirit to an inconspicuous area of the wall. If the spirit does not stain, moisten the cloth with white spirit and lightly dab the spot or stain. Allow to dry.

⚠ Warning

Don't use white spirit near heat or flame. Always allow proper ventilation.

Things You'll Need

☐ soft rags or vacuum cleaner

☐ wood cleaner and soft cloth

☐ white spirit (optional)

Clean and Care for Marble

Marble isn't as tough as you may think; it's a comparatively soft stone which is easily scratched and marred. Chances are you paid a lot for it, so keep it clean and take good care of it.

◎Steps

1 Wipe down marble surfaces with a damp rag and polish dry with a chamois for routine weekly cleaning.

2   Use a neutral, non-abrasive cleaner (such as acetone, hydrogen peroxide or clear ammonia) for tough stains.

3   Apply the cleaner with a cloth and polish dry.

4   After cleaning, polish marble surfaces using a marble polish containing tin oxide.

5   Protect marble floors with a stone sealer, and use standard non-abrasive floor cleaners to clean them.

6   Place coasters under glasses and put plastic under cosmetics on marble surfaces. Use rugs to cover marble floors.

7   Refer scratches of any depth to a professional.

⚠ Warnings

Powdered cleansers will scratch or damage marble.

Even weak acids – vinegar, wine, orange juice, cola – can damage marble, so make sure that you mop up spills immediately and rinse with water.

Things You'll Need

☐ rags and chamois

☐ cleaner

☐ marble polish

☐ stone sealer

☐ floor cleaner

123

Water Houseplants

More houseplants die from too much water than from not enough. Here's how to determine when your plants need water.

⊙ Steps

1   Poke your finger right into the soil, 2–3 cm (1 in) below the surface or up to your first knuckle. If the soil feels dry to the touch below the

surface, it's time to water. If it feels damp, wait a day or two and test again.

2 Use an inexpensive moisture meter to check the moisture level in the soil as an alternative to the fingertip test.

3 Provide extra water for plants that require moist soil, such as ferns and philodendrons. The soil should feel like a wrung-out sponge.

4 Use self-watering pots if you don't have the time to check your plants daily. These handy pots allow the plants to help themselves to a drink. You will need to check the pots' water reservoirs every two weeks.

5 Use tepid or warm water for tropical plants. Allow the water to sit in the watering can overnight to warm to room temperature. For lime-hating plants use tap water or distilled water.

6 Mist plants frequently. They do take in moisture through their leaves, and the humidity mimics their tropical environment.

7 Avoid watering too much in winter when plants are dormant. Water more often once they start into active growth in spring.

✴ Tips

Plants in bright light will use more water than those in low-light areas.

Make a humidity tray by placing gravel in the saucer. When you water, moisture will evaporate from the gravel up through the foliage.

⚠ Warning

Never allow plants to sit in standing water. Drain saucers half an hour after watering.

124

Feed Houseplants

You need to feed houseplants during their growing season, which is spring and summer.

⊙ Steps

1 Select a liquid fertiliser formulated for houseplants, and use it as directed during the growing season (spring and summer).

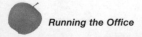

Running the Office

2 Add the concentrated fertiliser directly to the watering can.

3 Remove a plant from its saucer and place it in an area where water can run freely through the soil, such as in a sink or bath.

4 Pour the fertiliser solution onto the surface of the soil. Make sure it flows from the pot's drainage hole.

5 Allow the water to drain through the pot thoroughly before replacing the plant on its saucer.

6 Consider another method: use a slow-release fertiliser in the form of granules or spikes. Apply the product according to label directions.

⚠ Warnings

Don't feed more than is recommended, or you may burn your plants or get a salt build-up on the terracotta pot.

Try not to get any fertiliser on the foliage; it may burn the leaves and cause spots.

Things You'll Need

❏ liquid fertiliser

❏ watering can

❏ slow-release fertiliser

125

Stock an Emergency Supply of Medicine and First Aid

When an injury occurs, having medical materials within easy reach can help minimise bleeding, swelling and trauma. That's why every office should possess a well-stocked first aid kit.

⊙ Steps

1 Buy a plastic storage container that is shoe box size or larger – a fishing-tackle box will work nicely. Think of this container as the "safe box" for your emergency supplies.

2   Gather materials necessary to treat cuts and lacerations: a selection of wrapped plasters, sterile plain and non-stick gauze pads in a variety of sizes, bandages, soft bandage wraps and a pair of latex gloves for the care of fresh bleeding wounds (caution: some people are allergic to latex).

3   Soap or liquid antiseptic disinfectant for use in cleaning wounds. Soap containing chlorhexidine makes a good antiseptic. Have some antiseptic wipes if access to water may be a problem.

4   Skin closure strips or butterfly bandages to hold the sides of a wound together.

5   Include at least two sizes of bandage tape, and crêpe bandage or tubigrip to hold gauze pads or other dressings in place. Crêpe bandage and tubigrip can aso be used to support sprains and strains.

6   Place tubes of analgesic and antihistamine cream in the kit.

7   Burn dressings.

8   A triangular bandage to use as a sling.

9   Oral rehydration mixture to use after a bout of diarrhoea.

10 A thermometer.

11 Supplies of a pain killer such as Paracetamol, aspirin (not to be given to children under 12) or Ibuprofen.

12 Consider keeping an aqueous epinephrine solution kit (called an EpiPen) in the box if anyone is allergic to bees or wasps. You will need a prescription for the kit. Review how to use the kit with everyone who might need to know.

13 Put a good pair of tweezers and a pair of sharp scissors in the kit. The tweezers are great for removing gravel from scraped knees, as well as splinters and pieces of glass. The sharp scissors can quickly cut away a trouser leg from a lacerated thigh.

14 Include a bottle of sterile eye-irrigating solution.

15 Put a torch with fresh batteries in the kit, and be sure to check the batteries every few months. Good light is vital for detecting foreign bodies in the eyes, mouth and ears, and in assessing the depth and severity of wounds.

16 Keep a first aid manual inside the kit. Review the manual every six months so you'll remember what to do in an emergency.

17 Enrol on a first aid course for optimal emergency preparedness. These are available at most adult education institutes.

Tip

Add a flannel and towel (in a sterile plastic bag) to your kit when you travel. Most wounds can be cleaned effectively with soap and clean water, as long as the flannel and towel are also clean.

⚠ Warnings

Read and follow all instructions on packaging.

Inspect your kit once a year and replace any expired medication.

Keep first aid kits in a cool, dark place, out of reach of children.

Things You'll Need

- ☐ plastic storage container
- ☐ a selection of wrapped plasters
- ☐ sterile plain gauze pads
- ☐ sterile non-stick gauze pads
- ☐ soft bandage wrap
- ☐ latex gloves
- ☐ soap or liquid antiseptic disinfectant
- ☐ antiseptic wipes
- ☐ skin closure strips or butterfly bandages
- ☐ bandages and bandage tape
- ☐ crêpe bandage or tubigrip
- ☐ analgesic and antihistamine cream
- ☐ burn dressings
- ☐ triangular bandage
- ☐ oral rehydration mixture
- ☐ thermometer
- ☐ pain killers
- ☐ epinephrine kit (EpiPen)
- ☐ tweezers and sharp scissors
- ☐ sterile eye-irrigating solution
- ☐ torch and batteries
- ☐ first aid manual

First Aid

Stop a Nosebleed

Nosebleeds are caused by broken blood vessels inside the nose and are especially common in children. They usually go away on their own but will stop more quickly with help.

◉ Steps

1 Pinch your nose between your thumb and forefinger, and apply moderate pressure by squeezing against the nasal septum – the midsection of your nose – for 15 minutes.

2 Lean your head forwards, not backwards, so that the blood does not trickle down your throat. This will prevent a feeling of gagging.

3 Breathe through your mouth.

4 Apply a cold, soft compress around your nose as you continue to pinch it between your fingers.

5 Once bleeding has stopped, elevate your head above your heart when you are lying in bed or on the sofa. This helps alleviate nasal pressure.

6 Turn on a cool vaporiser to moisten mucus membranes, which will help prevent the nosebleed from recurring.

7 Apply a small amount of petroleum jelly to the inside of the nostrils to moisten the passages and prevent the nosebleed from recurring. Use your fingertip.

8 Avoid blowing your nose for 24 hours, and when you do blow it again, blow gently.

9 Avoid lifting heavy objects or engaging in other strenuous activities after a nosebleed. This can produce momentary surges in blood pressure that could cause the nose to bleed again.

✳ Tips

Anterior (in the front) nosebleeds are the everyday kind. Posterior (in the back) nosebleeds involve heavy bleeding from deep within the nose and are much more difficult to stop. Posterior nosebleeds occur most often in the elderly.

Keep your child's fingernails trimmed if she likes to poke around in her nose.

⚠ Warning

Seek medical care if your nose continues bleeding after 20 minutes, if the bleeding worsens rather than improves, or if you have specific medical conditions or concerns.

127

Care for Minor Cuts and Abrasions

Treating a cut right away reduces the chance of infection.

◉ Steps

1. Wash your hands before and after tending a wound.

2. Rinse the wound with clean water. Flush out all dirt and debris.

3. Using clean gauze, put pressure on the wound to stop any bleeding.

4. Clean the area around the injury with soap (or liquid antiseptic) and water or antiseptic wipes. Avoid getting any solution inside the wound.

5. Leave the wound open to the air unless there is a chance that you'll be exposing it to dirt or infection. In that case, bandage the wound loosely, allowing air to get in.

6. If the wound edges are open, use a butterfly bandage – a butterfly-shaped plaster that brings the edges of the wound together and reduces scarring – to close straight, clean, superficial wounds.

7. Call your doctor if you detect signs of infection, which include redness, warmth, redness up the arm, or oozing or drainage from the wound.

⚠ Warning

See a doctor if the wound is deep, won't stop bleeding or has edges that won't come together. Animal bites, human bites and deep wounds should be evaluated by a doctor in case antibiotics are needed. Also see a doctor if the wound is very dirty and it has been more than ten years since your last tetanus injection.

Things You'll Need

☐ soap, liquid antiseptic or antiseptic wipes

☐ gauze

☐ plasters

Remove a Splinter

Splinters can cause pain, swelling and possibly infection if they're not removed promptly.

⊙ Steps

1   Try to "milk" out the splinter by gently squeezing your fingertips over or on each side of it. If this doesn't work, try the following steps.

2   If you're worried about causing pain, rub the splinter site with a numbing teething gel or ice before removing the splinter. Keep in mind, however, that chilling the area may cause the splinter to retract from the top of the skin and may make its removal more challenging.

3   Clean a needle, a pair of tweezers and a small pair of nail clippers with isopropyl alcohol or liquid antiseptic solution and let it air-dry. Be sure to swab the pinching surfaces of the tweezers and the cutting edges of the nail clippers.

4   Use soap and water, or a liquid antiseptic solution, to wash the skin where the splinter has lodged.

5   With the tip of the needle, make a small hole in the skin above the splinter. Once you have access to the splinter, gently try to squeeze it through the hole. If necessary, increase the size of the hole with the needle. Use your tweezers to pull out the splinter as soon as you can get hold of it.

6   If you're not able to open a path for the splinter with the needle, use the nail clippers very carefully to cut away the skin above the splinter.

7   Wipe the site with isopropyl alcohol or a liquid antiseptic solution when you've removed the splinter.

8   Apply an antiseptic ointment to the site.

✳ Tips

Soak the infected area in warm water to soften the skin if you have trouble getting access to the splinter.

Most splinters eventually work themselves out on their own.

⚠ Warnings

Do not dig at a splinter for longer than five minutes. If you're unable to remove it within that time, leave it alone, or see a doctor if you feel you are at risk of infection. Too much poking and prodding will lead to tissue damage.

Be sure you are up to date with your tetanus injections. Once you've had your initial injection, you need to get a booster every ten years. If a splinter comes in contact with earth or animal dung before it punctures your skin, it could be carrying the bacterium that causes tetanus.

129

Soothe a Burnt Tongue

That coffee just smelled too good to wait for it to cool, didn't it? Now it's time to give your burnt tongue about 24 hours to heal.

ⓘ Steps

1 Remember that the surfaces of your mouth and tongue are mucus membranes, and as such, they heal faster than other areas of your body. So even though your tongue may really hurt, be comforted in knowing that by tomorrow, the burn should be gone.

2 Cool your tongue with a frozen dessert such as ice cream or sorbet. Let the treat linger on top of your tongue before you swallow it. For severe burns, frozen foods can be left on top of the tongue for three to four minutes, until the tongue becomes slightly numb and the pain is dulled.

3 Suck on an ice cube. Don't bite down on the cube, though, because it can crack your teeth.

4 Inhale air through your mouth, across and over your tongue. The cool breeze will help relieve some of the sting.

5 Suck on a cough drop containing phenol, which helps numb the tongue's surface.

6 Talk to your doctor about prescription medication that you could apply to your tongue to numb it and completely relieve the pain.

7 Avoid using mouthwash or harsh toothpaste until the burn heals.

8 Do not eat oranges, pineapple and other acidic foods until your tongue stops hurting.

⚠ Warning

Contact a doctor if you have suffered a serious burn – blistering or severe pain – to your tongue.

130

Make a Sling

A sling is used to support an injured arm, wrist or hand. Making a proper sling requires a bandage, but if you don't have one, available articles of clothing can offer an alternative.

⊙ Steps

1 Make a triangular bandage, if you do not have one ready-made, by taking a piece of material at least 1 m (3 ft) square and cutting it in half diagonally from corner to corner.

2 Sit the injured person down and have them support their damaged arm with their other hand, so the forearm is across their chest with the hand slightly higher than the elbow.

3 Slide one tip of the triangular bandage upwards between the patient's chest and their injured arm.

4 Pull the bandage up, over the shoulder of the sound arm, and around the neck, so that the tip is pointing downwards on the injured side.

5 Take hold of the lower end of the bandage and fold it up over the injured forearm and hand, leaving only the fingertips showing.

6 Tie the ends of the bandage together in the hollow of the collarbone.

7 Check that the sling is not inhibiting circulation in the injured arm. To do this, press one of the patient's fingernails with your thumb until the nail turns white. Then release the pressure. The nail should become pink again. If it does not, adjust the sling until circulation is restored.

8   Place some soft padding under the knot if it is pressing uncomfortably
    on the patient's skin.

 Tips

Always stand on the injured side of the casualty when you apply a sling.
Then you will be better able to help support the injured arm while making
the sling.

You can improvise a sling using a scarf, a belt, a tie or even a pair of
tights, looped under the injured arm and tied around the patient's neck.
Alternatively, if the casualty is wearing a coat, pin the sleeve, with the
injured arm inside, to the front of the coat.

✓ 131 Recognise Signs of a Medical Emergency

Urgent medical attention is required for a number of medical conditions, including those whose common signs and symptoms are listed below. Call a doctor or visit the nearest hospital's accident and emergency department immediately if any of these occur, even if you are not entirely sure that it is an emergency.

Appendicitis

❑ Is the patient between the ages of 10 and 30? The condition is most common in this age group but can occur at any age.

❑ Is there pain and/or tenderness in the navel area that moves towards the lower right of the abdomen over the course of a few hours?

❑ Does the patient describe the pain as severe and sharp, and worsening with any movement?

❑ Is there a fever? This may be a sign of inflammation and infection, a possible sign of appendicitis.

❑ Is the patient experiencing signs of nausea, vomiting or loss of appetite?

❑ Did the patient take any pain medicine that may mask the symptoms of appendicitis?

Heart attack

❑ Is there crushing pain, pressure or squeezing in the centre of the chest that lasts for more than a few minutes?

❑ Does the pain spread to the jaw, neck, shoulders, back or arms (often the left arm)?

❑ Is there any nausea, sweating, dizziness or shortness of breath in combination with chest pain?

❑ Is the person over 50 and experiencing indigestion or heartburn that does not respond to over-the-counter medication?

❑ Is there a combination of these symptoms?

chechlist

Anaphylactic shock

❑ Has the patient been exposed within the last two hours to a common allergen, such as an insect sting, nuts, peanuts, seeds, legumes, eggs or shellfish? A person may be allergic to any of these even if he or she has been exposed to them before without problems.

❑ Does the patient report tingling in the mouth and tongue and/or throbbing ears?

❑ Does the patient appear uneasy or agitated?

❑ Does the patient's skin appear flushed and feel itchy, and are hives appearing on the skin or swellings becoming evident on the eyes, lips or tongue?

❑ Is the patient sneezing, coughing, wheezing or having difficulty breathing?

❑ Is the patient vomiting or experiencing abdominal cramps or diarrhoea?

Stroke

❑ Is there any numbness or weakness on one side of the body such as in one arm or leg, or on one side of the face?

❑ Is the person having problems such as difficulty speaking or a loss of speech altogether?

❑ Are there any vision problems such as double vision or loss of vision, especially if this occurs in just one eye?

❑ Is there any sign of sudden, severe, unexplained headaches, dizziness, loss of coordination or balance, or sudden falling without apparent cause?

checklist

Care for a Toothache

Toothache symptoms include throbbing pain around a certain tooth, sensitivity to hot or cold, and discomfort when chewing. Causes vary from cavities and gum disease to cracked teeth and exposed roots.

⊙ Steps

1 Clean your mouth by rinsing it with warm water.

2 Floss gently around the sensitive tooth to dislodge any food particles.

3 Try placing an ice pack on your jaw to soothe the pain.

4 Use over-the-counter painkillers such as aspirin (for adults only) or ibuprofen to relieve the pain, or talk to a pharmacist about topical analgesic ointments.

5 Call your dentist if you have a fever or if the pain worsens, is recurrent or lasts for more than a few hours. Your dentist will ask you questions to determine the urgency of your need for treatment.

6 Prevent future toothaches with good oral hygiene. Brush twice a day with a fluoride toothpaste, floss once daily and see your dentist for check-ups every six months.

✱ Tip

Some people find relief by chewing on cloves – if you can't find a clove, look for oil of cloves as the main ingredient in a pain reliever.

⚠ Warning

Never put aspirin or other painkillers directly on or around the sore tooth unless they are specifically designed to be used this way; some products can burn your mouth.

Avoid a Cold

The common cold is caused by any one of more than 200 viruses. Symptoms can include a fever, watery eyes, nasal congestion, a runny nose, sneezing, a sore throat and a cough.

⊙ Steps

1. Wash your hands often. Cold viruses can be transmitted by handshakes and by touching contaminated objects such as doorknobs.

2. Keep your hands away from your eyes, nose and mouth.

3. Avoid people who are coughing and/or sneezing.

4. Get plenty of rest to help strengthen your immune system.

5. Maintain a healthy diet and get an adequate amount of exercise.

6. Drink plenty of fluids.

7. Consider taking one 500 mg tablet of vitamin C twice a day. Some scientists believe this can help boost your immune system, although there is no hard data to support this.

✷ Tips

Some studies have shown that the herbal supplement echinacea may be effective at fighting cold symptoms when taken during the first few days of illness – but not prior to exposure. However, there is no scientific data that supports the effectiveness of echinacea.

You may be more susceptible to colds when you are under stress, during your menstrual period, or when you are old – times when your immune system is weakened.

Prevent the Flu

Maintaining a healthy immune system is your best bet for avoiding the flu (short for influenza). Here are some simple ways to support your system through the flu season.

◉ Steps

1 Avoid sharing drinking and eating utensils with people who are sick.

2 Wash your hands before eating – it really does help keep germs away.

3 Increase your vitamin C intake – which may boost your immune system – by eating ample amounts of fresh fruits and vegetables. Oranges, tomatoes and broccoli are good choices.

4 Drink at least eight glasses of water a day. Herbal teas and diluted fruit juices are good options for increasing your water intake.

5 Get enough sleep. Most people need at least seven to eight hours a night for optimal rest.

6 Manage your stress. Chronic stress can weaken the immune system.

7 Take a multivitamin tablet every day to make sure you are getting enough vitamins and minerals.

8 Exercise regularly – it's been shown to reduce the occurrence of colds and flu.

✳ Tips

Flu injections are available and particularly recommended for high-risk groups, such as those with immune disorders and anyone over the age of 65.

Some studies have shown that the herbal supplement echinacea may be effective at fighting flu symptoms when taken during the first few days of illness – but not prior to exposure. However, there is no scientific data that supports the effectiveness of echinacea.

Too much vitamin C can cause diarrhoea and gastric discomfort. Avoid taking more than 500 mg of vitamin C twice a day.

Relieve a Sore Throat

Sore throats can be caused by bacteria or a virus and often accompany an illness such as a cold or flu. Most require no medical intervention and will go away in two or three days.

⊙ Steps

1 Consider the cause: a bug that's going around the office, enthusiastic cheering, or perhaps something more serious, such as a throat infection.

2 Take an analgesic to reduce inflammation – aspirin, paracetamol or ibuprofen for an adult, or paracetamol or ibuprofen for children – as recommended by your doctor.

3 Suck on throat lozenges if you are an adult – especially those containing menthol, benzocaine or phenol, which numb the throat. Children should suck on cough drops or hard sweets.

4 Gargle with mint mouthwash or salt water.

5 Spray a throat spray containing numbing agents into the back of your throat, if you are an adult.

6 Brush your tongue. Sometimes, removing the build-up on your tongue can lessen the soreness in your throat.

7 Rinse your toothbrush in mouthwash between brushings to kill bacteria.

8 Drink ice-cold beverages. Try filling a glass half-full of crushed ice; then pour fruit juice over the ice. Let it sit for ten minutes, insert a straw and suck slowly, letting the juice rest a minute on the back of your throat.

9 Add moisture to your environment with a humidifier or vaporiser, or sit in a steamy shower or bath.

10 Eat soft or liquid foods, especially sorbets and chicken broth.

11 Avoid cigarette smoke and other airborne irritants.

✷ Tip

Ask your chemist to recommend a good lozenge or throat spray.

First Aid

⚠ Warnings

For a severe sore throat accompanied by fever, difficulty swallowing or breathing, a red rash, or coughing up of brown sputum, see your doctor or go immediately to the nearest hospital's accident and emergency department.

Contact a doctor if you have a sore throat that keeps you from being able to swallow.

Check young children for dribbling. Dribbling indicates trouble swallowing, which can lead to difficulty in breathing and requires immediate medical attention.

136

Get Rid of Hiccups

The cause and function of these abrupt diaphragmatic contractions have always baffled medical practitioners, but a few home remedies can help get rid of them.

⊙ Steps

1   Swallow 1 tsp white granulated sugar, dry. A study found that this stopped hiccups immediately in 19 out of 20 people. Repeat up to three more times at two-minute intervals if necessary.

2   Gulp down a glass of water if the sugar doesn't work.

3   Eat a piece of dry bread slowly.

4   Breathe in and out of a paper bag. Do not use a plastic bag under any circumstances, and don't do this longer than one minute.

5   Gargle with water.

6   Repeat the above steps until your hiccups stop.

✴ Tip

Hiccups can be brought on by eating too fast and subsequently swallowing a lot of air, or by drinking too much alcohol.

137

🏃 🏃 🏃

Fit Exercise Into Your Busy Schedule

Make a commitment to exercise every day if you can. Try to
get in at least 30 minutes of walking or more vigorous
exercise.

◎ Steps

1   Try walking, cycling or roller-blading to work. If this takes longer than
    your usual commute, plan ahead: pack your briefcase and lay out your
    clothes the night before. Keep a change of clothes at work if need be.

2   If an alternative commute is impossible, get off the bus a little earlier
    and walk the rest of the way, park at the far end of the car park, or
    take the stairs instead of the lift.

3   Make use of your lunch break. Play a quick game of squash, make a
    speedy gym visit, go for a jog or take a brisk walk (use some light
    hand weights for a bonus workout).

4   Stretch at your desk. This reduces muscle tension, gets your
    circulation moving and prepares you for more strenuous activity later.

5   Do some chores. Mow the lawn or rake the leaves for 20 minutes.
    Housework burns calories, and you have to get the work done
    anyway.

6   Play games with your children. Kick a football or play some
    hopscotch.

✳ Tips

New mums can join an aerobics class specially designed for them and
their babies. You can network with other mums, stay fit and keep an eye
on the baby, who gets involved as part of your workout routine.

Exercise with a friend – you can motivate one another.

Carry a notebook and keep a record of your activities and their duration. Increase your daily exercise as time goes on.

⚠ Warning

Always consult your doctor before beginning an exercise programme.

138

Exercise at Your Office

You may not want to turn your office into a gym, but there are exercises you can do at or near your desk to boost your energy level, relieve stress and burn calories.

⊙ Steps

1 Try some squats. Stand in front of your chair with your feet shoulder-width apart. Bend your knees as though you're sitting on the chair, keeping your weight on your heels. When your legs are parallel with the seat of the chair, slowly rise to your original standing position.

2 Hold up the wall with wall sits. Stand with your back touching the wall. Move your feet away from the wall so that the wall is supporting the weight of your back. Bend your knees so that your legs form a 90-degree angle. Hold as long as you can.

3 Pose like a warrior – with a lunge. With your arms by your sides, take a giant step forwards with your right leg so your thigh is parallel with the floor. Pushing off the same leg, return to your starting position. Repeat with the left leg. (Travelling lunges are also an option if you have room – keep moving forwards with each lunge.)

4 Try calf raises during a coffee break. Holding on to your desk or a filing cabinet for balance, raise your heels off the floor, then lower them.

5 Peek into your neighbour's cubicle while you do toe raises. Sitting in your chair or standing, lift and lower your toes while keeping your heels on the ground, or walk around on the heels of your feet.

6 Burn that bottom with a gluteal squeeze. While sitting or standing, squeeze the muscles of your rear end. Hold, then relax.

7 Get on the floor and do some crunches. Lying on your back with your knees bent, reach for your knees, hold for two counts, then return to the floor. No need to curl all the way up – stop when your abdominal muscles are fully contracted; your shoulders will be just a few inches off the floor.

8 Do some push-ups, standing upright and pushing against a wall with your hands a little wider than shoulder-width apart, or lying face down on the ground.

9 Do some dips. Sitting on your chair, with the palms of your hands on your chair and feet on the floor, scoot your rear end off the end of the seat. Bend your elbows, lowering your body, then straighten your arms to return to the starting position.

10 Release tension with shoulder raises. Raise your shoulders up to your ears, hold, then relax.

✱ Tips

Doing squats will help protect your knees from future injuries. However, if you've had a knee injury in the past, check with your doctor about what exercises are appropriate for you, and go easy when trying any new exercises involving the knee.

If you're not familiar with strength-training exercises, seek the assistance of a qualified personal trainer or a physiotherapist to get you started properly.

Always warm up or begin exercising gradually.

Perform enough repetitions of each exercise to feel fatigue in the muscles being worked.

It helps to have comfortable clothes on hand or to work for a company that observes a casual dress code.

⚠ Warnings

Use discretion in the workplace: Do only what's appropriate for your particular work environment.

If using a chair to perform exercises, be sure to choose a sturdy, supportive one without wheels.

Self Improvement

Stay Motivated to Exercise

You know you should exercise, but some days it's tough to get moving. Discover what motivates you, and use these strategies to develop and maintain an active lifestyle.

⊙ Steps

1 Determine an attainable goal, such as exercising twice during the week and once on weekends. Creating realistic goals will set you up for success. If your goal becomes too easy, you can always design a more ambitious one.

2 Devise rewards for achieving your goal. The reward can be a massage, a new workout outfit, a new CD, a session with a personal trainer or that hardcover novel you've had your eye on – whatever you really want.

3 Partner with a friend, co-worker or loved one – someone who will support you and your goals without sabotaging them.

4 Subscribe to a fitness magazine or online fitness newsletter. New tips and exercises can be inspirational and alleviate boredom.

5 Create a competition with co-workers or friends. For example, the team whose members exercise for 30 minutes, three times each week, for two months wins a prize.

6 Change into your workout clothes. Sometimes, just getting dressed is the biggest barrier.

7 Erase the concept that if you can't do at least 30 minutes you're wasting your time. Even in small doses, exercise burns calories, increases energy and improves your health.

8 Try a new sport or class. Adding variety, group support and competition can increase your likelihood of exercising.

9 Make a commitment to your dog or your neighbour's dog to go for a long walk at least twice each week.

10 Look for ways to incorporate activity into your day, even if you can't do your normal exercise routine. Take the stairs instead of the lift, go bowling instead of to the cinema, or use a push mower instead of a powered electric mower.

11 Sign up for a race and send in the entry fee. Whatever your activity –
running, cycling, walking, swimming – there are hundreds of races
offered all over the world. Pick a place you've always wanted to visit.

12 Join a gym or health club. For some, paying for a membership
increases the likelihood of compliance. It also eliminates the bad-
weather excuse.

✱ Tips

Exercise in the morning. Research shows that people who make exercise
a priority first thing in the day are more likely to stick with it.

Every person goes through periods when it's very challenging to
maintain an exercise programme. Acknowledge it when it happens,
recognise that it's just a brief period of time, and restart your programme
as soon as possible.

Choose things that motivate you – not what others want.

Remind yourself of the many health benefits of an exercise programme.

140
Break a Bad Habit

Habits such as biting your nails, downing large amounts of
caffeine and even gossiping are automatic behaviours that
can be changed with patience and persistence.

⊙ Steps

1 Decide how serious you are about breaking the habit. In addition to a
strong commitment, you'll need time and energy to pay attention to
your behaviour so you can change it.

2 Keep track of the behaviour. Keep a notepad or journal handy.

3 Write down when it happens (what the overall situation is when it
occurs) and what you were thinking and feeling. Writing increases your
awareness of when and why you have this habit.

4 Read and think about what you write down. What does this habit do
for you? Is it a way to deal with feelings of boredom, anxiety, stress or
anger?

5. Think of what you could do instead of the habit that would be a more positive way to deal with the feelings or situations that provoke it. Write down some simple alternative behaviours. Pick one you want to practise.

6. Try to catch yourself when you find yourself indulging in the habit, and stop yourself as soon as you can. Start the alternative behaviour you decided you wanted to do instead.

7. Aim to do this once a week at first, then increase the number of times per week over time. The more you practise a new behaviour, the more it becomes the new habit.

8. Get support from others by letting them know you are working on the habit and telling them what they can do to help.

 Tips

Be patient with yourself. Habits are so automatic and unconscious, you may not even realise you're engaging in the behaviour until you're already doing it.

Be kind to yourself. Browbeating yourself is another bad habit to be broken.

141
Stop Smoking

You've probably already heard the many reasons why you should stop smoking – now check out the various ways of how to go about it.

⊙ **Steps**

1. Ask yourself why you want to stop smoking.

2. Write your answers on a piece of paper and carry it with you.

3. Whenever you feel like smoking, use your list to remind yourself of why you want to stop.

4. Fill out a "stop smoking contract". Sign it, and have a family member or friend sign it as a witness.

5. Throw away all your cigarettes, lighters and ashtrays.

Office Life

6   Change your schedule to avoid circumstances in which you usually smoke. Walk around the block or chew gum when you would normally be smoking.

7   Put up no-smoking signs in your house, your work area and your car.

8   Prepare yourself to feel the urge to start smoking again. Here are four ways to deal with the urge to smoke: delaying, deep breathing, drinking water and doing something else.

9   Carry around "mouth toys" – sweets, chewing gum, straws, carrot sticks.

10 List the good things that have happened since you stopped smoking, and keep the list with you as an inspiration wherever you go. For example, you might note that your breath is fresher, you can climb the stairs without getting out of breath, and you've saved enough money to buy a new DVD player.

11 Reward yourself for stopping smoking; for example, you could take the money you have saved and buy yourself something nice.

✳ Tips

Ask your doctor about nicotine products and other types of medication if you have tried unsuccessfully to stop in the past.

Be prepared to persist despite a few relapses.

Planning meals, eating a healthful diet and staying active will help you maintain your weight.

Look for a support group or smoking-cessation class.

⚠ Warning

You may experience irritability, depression or a dry mouth due to nicotine withdrawal after you stop smoking. These symptoms should pass.

142

Stop Worrying

The keys to worrying less are to challenge your worrisome thoughts and to calm yourself physically and emotionally.

⊙ Steps

1   Write down what you are worried about. Include your imagined worst-case scenarios.

2   Think about how you would handle your worst-case scenarios.

3   Decide what actions you could take that would change the situation and give you less to worry about. Then follow through on those actions.

4   Try to think logically about the worrisome thoughts that you feel you can't take any action on. Consider which of them are excessive or distorted and have very little basis in reality.

5   For each of these worrisome thoughts, write down an alternative way of looking at the problem that presents a rational challenge to your worries.

6   Try to catch yourself when you notice that you're becoming overwhelmed with worry. Stop and remind yourself of the alternative way to look at the situation.

7   Practise relaxation and stress-reduction techniques. One simple thing you can do to help quiet your mind and calm your emotions and body is to breathe in slowly and deeply to the count of six and breathe out slowly to the count of six. Do this for five minutes; gradually increase to 20 minutes over time.

8   Learn to accept what you cannot change or have no power to control in life. Read books dealing with worry, anxiety, acceptance and inner peace. Look in the psychology, self-help and spirituality sections of your bookshop or library.

✱ Tips

If you need to, get help from others in coming up with challenges to your worrisome thoughts. They can often present you with a different perspective on things.

Many people find spiritual teachings or belief in a higher power extremely helpful in decreasing worry and developing more trust in life.

⚠ Warning

Seek professional help if your worries are interfering with your daily functioning or causing you significant distress.

Office Life

Be Happy

Happiness has different meanings for everyone; we each have to define and seek it for ourselves.

◎Steps

1 Decide what is important to you in life. For example: Do you value a certain kind of job; material things; a relationship; time alone or with others; time to relax or to be creative; time to read, listen to music or have fun? These are just a few of the possibilities.

2 Think about times when you have felt happy, good, or content. Where were you? Whom were you with? What were you doing, thinking or experiencing that made you feel happy?

3 Decide to make more time in your life to do more of what is important to you and makes you feel happier. To be happy, you have to make happiness a priority in your life.

4 Start with little things and work up to bigger ones. Little things might include reading an engrossing book for 15 minutes; taking a walk; telephoning a friend; or buying scented soap, shampoo, candles or tea that you will enjoy every time you use them.

5 Focus on what is positive about yourself, others and life in general instead of dwelling on the negative. Write down as many positive things as you can think of in a journal. Keep it handy to read over and continue adding to it.

6 Appreciate what is working in your life at the moment. In the major areas of your life, such as your health, job, love life, friends, family, money and living situation, what is going well?

✳Tips

Ask other people, "What makes you happy?" or "What is something that makes you feel good?"

It's OK to ask for professional help. Talk to someone, such as a psychotherapist, career counsellor or spiritual adviser (minister or teacher) to help you sort out what would make you happy.

Read books on the subject of happiness. Wise people have been writing about it for hundreds of years. In the bookshop, look under psychology, spirituality, or philosophy.

Self-improvement

Overcome Shyness

Everyone feels shy sometimes, but being too shy can hamper many aspects of your life.

⊙ Steps

1 Determine why you're shy in the first place. For example, are you afraid of what someone might say about your physical appearance? Remember, there's an underlying reason for how you react in situations.

2 Act as if you're not shy. In private, behave as if you're oozing confidence. Hold your chin up, stand up straight and tall, stride confidently and speak firmly. It may seem ridiculous, but you will see results when you're out in public.

3 Practise making eye contact and smiling when you have interactions with others. Strike up casual conversations with strangers about the weather or current events.

4 Look your best. One way to reduce self-consciousness is to always look good and limit opportunities for being self-critical.

5 Decrease your fear of rejection by imagining the worst possible outcome. If you approach someone, he or she may say no to your overture or may just walk away. Everybody has been rejected at some point, but no one has to dwell on it.

6 Look and learn. Watching friends or even strangers who aren't shy is a good way to learn some tips first-hand.

7 Develop a positive feeling about yourself, don't get frustrated, and have fun. Keep in mind that the real goal is to meet people who will like you for who you are.

✱ Tip

Find out about progressive relaxation techniques. These same steps can be applied to situations that cause you to feel shy.

Introduce People

Want to meet new people and improve your social and business graces? Here's how to make proper introductions at business functions, parties, dinners and other social situations.

⊙ **Steps**

1 Introduce individuals to each other using both first and last names.

2 If you're introducing someone who has a title – a doctor, for example – include the title as well as the first and last names in the introduction.

3 Introduce the younger or less prominent person to the older or more prominent person, regardless of the sex of the individuals. (However, if a considerable age difference lies between the two, it is far more courteous to make introductions in deference to age, regardless of social rank.) For example: "Arthur Dent, I'd like you to meet Dr Gertrude Smith."

4 If the person you are introducing has a specific relationship to you, make the relationship clear by adding a phrase such as "my boss", "my wife" or "my uncle". In the case of unmarried couples who are living together, "companion" and "partner" are good choices.

5 Use your spouse's first and last name if he or she has a different last name than you. Include the phrase "my wife" or "my husband".

6 Introduce an individual to the group first, then the group to the individual. For example: "Dr Brown, I'd like you to meet my friends Kim Howe, Simon Campbell and Michael Vince. Everyone, this is Dr Kurt Brown."

✱ **Tips**

If you've forgotten a name, you'll seem impolite if you try to ignore the need for the introduction. It's less awkward (and better manners) to apologise and acknowledge that the name has escaped you.

If your host neglects to introduce you to other guests, feel free to introduce yourself, but make your relationship to the host clear in your introduction.

Shake Hands

Historically used to show that both people were unarmed, the handshake today is a critical gauge of confidence, trust, sophistication and mood.

⊙ Steps

1 Extend your right hand to meet the other person's right hand.

2 Point your thumb upwards towards the other person's arm and extend your arm at a slight downward angle.

3 Wrap your hand around the other person's hand when your thumb joints come together.

4 Grasp the hand firmly and squeeze gently once. Remember that limp handshakes are a big turnoff, as are bone-crushing grasps.

5 Hold the handshake for two to three seconds.

6 Pump your hand up and down a few times to convey sincerity. (This gesture is optional.)

✱ Tip

A two-handed handshake is not for first meetings. It is a sign of real affection, and you should reserve it for friends and intimates.

⚠ Warning

Handshakes are not appropriate in all cultures. Investigate local customs if you will be visiting a foreign country.

Remember Names

The ability to remember the names of people you meet will always serve you well.

◎ Steps

1　Pay attention when you are introduced to someone. A few minutes after you meet the person, say his or her name to yourself again. If you have forgotten it, talk to the person again and ask for the name.

2　Write down the new name three times while picturing the person's face; do this as soon as possible after meeting someone.

3　Ask how to spell a difficult name, or glance at the spelling on the person's business card, if it's offered. If you know the spelling of a word and can picture it in your mind, you'll remember it better.

4　Connect a name to a common word you will remember. For example, the name Salazar could sound like "salamander", "bazaar" or "sell a jar".

5　Make a connection to the person's hobby or employment. "Bill the pill" might help you remember the name of a pharmacist, for example.

✳ Tip

Writing down new names is generally a very successful memorising technique that doesn't require a lot of work.

148

Be a Proper Guest at a Party

A good guest responds promptly to the invitation, arrives fashionably late, is cheerful and friendly, and isn't the last one to go home.

◎ Steps

1　Reply to the invitation in a timely manner. Use the method indicated: phone, post or e-mail.

2　Bring a friend only if you receive an invitation for you and a guest. Your hosts may have a food, budget or space limitation.

3　Go with the spirit of the party. If it's for a special occasion, such as a housewarming, bring a gift. If it's dressy, wear your glad rags. Costume required? Dig into your wardrobe and get creative.

4 Prepare. Read up on current events; think of a few good stories; recall a few films, books or plays. Try hard not to be shy or moody – for your host's sake, if not your own.

5 Arrive reasonably close to the starting time. The starting time for a cocktail party tends to be looser than it is for a dinner party, which requires punctuality. Fashionably late means no more than 30 minutes past the indicated time.

6 Seek out your host or hostess and say hello as soon as you arrive.

7 Make an effort to mix and mingle cheerfully. Don't just hide in a corner chatting with people you already know.

8 Know your alcohol limits and don't exceed them. Take into consideration your energy level, food intake and drink size. Nothing's ruder than ruining a party with inappropriate behaviour.

9 Treat your host's home as you would your own – no wet glasses on the furniture, no cigarettes ground out in the plants, no cocktail sticks on the floor. Don't smoke without asking permission.

10 Leave at a reasonable hour. Some hosts close the bar half an hour before they want the party to end. Take a hint when others start slipping on their coats.

11 Find your hosts to say thank you and good night personally. It's also thoughtful to call the next day and let your host know how much you enjoyed the event.

 ## Tips

If you know your hosts, you might call and ask about the dress code, if the invitation doesn't make it clear. Or ask another guest who's attending.

Unless it's clear that this is not necessary, bring something to drink, whether or not it's alcoholic.

⚠ Warning

Never arrive early; your hosts may not be ready to receive guests.

Leave a Party Graciously

Arriving at the party is the easy part. When you are ready to leave, exercise tact and always thank the host or hostess before you depart.

⊙ Steps

1 Wait until the host is not in conversation or caught in the middle of cooking or serving duties.

2 Express your gratitude for the invitation, and compliment the host on one particular aspect of the party.

3 Make a tentative reference to the next time you will see each other. For example, saying "We should get together for drinks soon" takes the emphasis off your departure.

4 Acknowledge everyone in the room, if possible. If the party is too large to permit this, express a parting gesture to those guests with whom you spent time talking.

5 Make your parting words short and sweet in an attempt to let everyone else get back to the festivities.

✱ Tips

Avoid long and effusive apologies. Others will look upon your departure negatively if you insist on apologising for it.

If the party invitation included an ending time, don't stay too long after the time indicated.

Tie a Tie

Once you've mastered the technique, you won't need a mirror to look dapper in your favourite tie. These instructions will teach you how to tie a four-in-hand knot.

⊙ Steps

1 Lift up the collar of your shirt and put the tie around the back of your neck. The wide end should hang down about twice as low as the thin end; it can hang closer to your right or left hand, depending on what's most comfortable for you.

2 Wrap the wide end around the thin end twice, a few inches below your neck. The wide end should go over the thin end at first.

3 After wrapping the wide end around the second time, push it up through the gap between your chin and the partially formed knot.

4 Tuck the wide end through the front loop of the knot.

5 Gently pull down on both the thin and wide ends below the knot until it is tight.

6 Hold the thin end and slide the knot up to your neck.

7 If the thin end hangs below the wide end, untie the tie and begin again, with the wide end hanging lower than it did the first time.

8 If the wide end hangs too low, untie the tie and begin again, with the wide end hanging higher than it did the first time.

9 Flip your collar back down once you and your tie look dapper.

✱ Tip

When untying a tie, follow the directions in reverse rather than just pulling the narrow end through the knot. Otherwise, you may distort the shape of the tie.

151

Buy a Man's Business Suit

Everyday business attire may have become more casual, but the suit is still the anchor of any man's formal wardrobe. Start with a classic navy suit and move on to grey, pinstripe or camel.

⊙ Steps

1   Choose a jacket style. The two-button, single-breasted jacket is a popular style, but three- or four-button jackets are also available. Keep in mind that fashions change for men's clothing, just as they do for women's. Only thin men should wear formal double-breasted jackets, which add bulk to the figure. These should be kept buttoned at all times, as the jacket hangs awkwardly otherwise.

2   Select a fabric colour and pattern. If you opt for a patterned fabric, check to see that patterns line up at shoulder and lapel seams.

3   Choose a fabric. High-quality worsted wool is the most seasonally versatile. Cotton and linen are good for summer wear. Avoid blends that are made with too much polyester, as they don't breathe well and may look cheap.

4   Crumple the fabric to make sure it bounces back instead of wrinkling, unless you've chosen a fabric that's meant to wrinkle, such as linen.

5   Select a trouser style. Pleats make trousers dressy and provide room for movement, while flat-front trousers are slimming. Turn-ups are formal, add weight to the suit and can make the legs seem shorter; trousers without turn-ups elongate the legs and are more informal.

6   Test the jacket for fit. Make sure the collar lies flat against the back of your neck and shows a 6-mm (¼-in) rim of shirt collar. Shoulders should be lightly padded and neither too boxy nor too sloped. Sleeves should reveal 6 to 12 mm (¼ to ½ in) of shirt cuff and fall 13 cm (5 in) above the tip of your thumb.

7   Button the jacket and sit down to verify that it is comfortable and doesn't bunch up.

8   Make sure the trousers sit on the waist, not hips, and drape over and break slightly at the tops of your shoes. Check that your socks aren't visible when you walk.

✳ Tips

Tall men should emphasise horizontal lines and avoid pinstripes. Double-breasted suits often flatter tall, thin men. Short men should consider single-breasted, shorter jackets in pinstripes or dark solids. Heavier men should also opt for pinstripes and avoid double-breasted suits.

When you buy a suit off the peg, you may have to take whichever trousers come with the jacket. If this is the case, the jacket style, which is more noticeable, should take precedence over the style of trousers. Keep in mind that turn-ups can be added to or removed from most pairs of trousers.

Buying a jacket and trousers separately will give you more style choices, and is a good approach if you need a special fit (if you have a large chest and a small waist, for example). It may be difficult to match the garments, though.

152

Dress Business Casual – Men

Many businesses allow somewhat casual attire at least once a week, but dress codes vary. Here are some guidelines for dressing business casual, which is a notch below business formal.

⊙ Steps

1 Ask your human resources department for official guidelines. Business casual means different things at different companies. At a large corporation, it may mean a sports jacket with a tie; at a smaller company, it may mean khaki trousers and a polo shirt.

2 Before you go casual, check your business diary to make sure you don't have any meetings that require formal business attire.

3 Select clean, pressed and wrinkle-free clothes. Your outfit should communicate professionalism.

4 Wear a collared shirt with a waistcoat. You can break up the ordinary cotton shirt monotony by wearing a linen or flannel shirt or one with a band collar. Knitted shirts and polo shirts are also generally acceptable. A casual sports jacket is appropriate.

5 Wear chinos, or khaki, corduroy or other non-denim trousers. Check your company's policy before you decide to wear jeans to work.

6 Be sure to wear a belt, and have it match the colour of your shoes.

7 Wear socks that match the colour of your trousers – leave white socks in your gym bag.

8   Choose oxfords, slip-ons, or rubber-soled leather shoes or boots for
     casual day. Wingtips are often too formal. Worn-out shoes, sandals or
     trainers won't do.

✱ Tips

Observe what others are wearing to get an idea of what is acceptable,
if your company has no written guidelines.

Your casual-day outfit should be formal enough that you can throw on
a sports jacket and meet a client.

⚠ Warning

Casual days generally do not include the option of not shaving.

153

Dress Business Casual – Women

Women can often get away with a wider range of attire than
men. Let comfort and professionalism guide you when you're
dressing for business casual occasions.

◎ Steps

1   Ask your human resources department for official guidelines. Business
     casual means different things at different companies. At a large
     corporation, it may mean trousers or a business skirt; at a smaller
     company, it may mean a cotton jumper and a floral skirt.

2   Before you go casual, check your business diary to make sure you
     don't have any meetings that require formal business attire.

3   Select clean, wrinkle-free clothes.

4   Wear a good-quality blouse or knitted top. Include a casual jacket or
     cardigan if appropriate.

5   Don pressed khakis or other trousers, or a dress or skirt. If a dress is
     sleeveless, wear a blazer or cardigan over it. Check your company's
     policy before you decide to wear jeans to work.

6   Wear shoes that are comfortable and appropriate for your outfit. Funky
     platform trainers or strappy sandals might be formal enough for some

companies; however, it's more typical to wear closed-toed leather shoes. Avoid worn-out shoes.

7　Keep the make-up light. Let your natural beauty shine through.

8　Accessorise with a silk scarf or classic bracelet to give your casual outfit a polished look.

Tips

A basic pair of black trousers is a must for any work wardrobe.

Business casual attire is more formal than weekend wear. Faded T-shirts, shorts, torn clothing and risqué attire are not appropriate.

154
Iron Trousers

Almost all trousers, apart from jeans, require ironing.

◉ Steps

1　Turn the trousers inside out. Look for the label that gives ironing and fabric information for the garment.

2　Choose the heat setting on your iron appropriate for that fabric. Linen and 100 per cent cotton take a high setting; wools and cotton blends call for medium heat; polyester, rayon, nylon, silk, acetate and acrylic all require a low heat setting.

3　Fill the iron with distilled (de-ionised) water if you will be using the steam setting on cotton or linen.

4　Test the iron on a small area to make sure you don't have the setting too high – this can damage or discolour the fabric.

5　With the trousers still inside out, iron the waistband, pockets (on both sides), fly area, seams and hems, in that order.

6　Turn the trousers right side out and pull the waistband over the pointed end of the board. Iron the waistband area and any pleats along the front of the trousers below the waistband.

7　Lay the trousers lengthwise along the ironing board with both legs together and carefully line up any pre-existing creases.

Office Life

8 Take the hem of the top trouser leg and bring it towards the waistband, folding the top leg away from the bottom leg. Iron the inside (hem to crotch) of the lower leg. Turn the trousers over and repeat for the other leg.

9 Smooth out both legs carefully and iron the outside of the top leg. Give extra attention to turn-ups, if the trousers have them.

10 Turn the trousers over and iron the outside of the other leg.

11 Hang warm trousers immediately to avoid wrinkling. Fold them through a suit hanger to avoid crushing them in a trouser hanger.

✳ Tips

The material in many suits can become shiny with too much ironing. You can avoid this by placing a clean cotton cloth over the area before ironing it.

Avoid spot-cleaning trousers just before ironing. Any wet spots may become permanent stains if ironed.

⚠ Warning

Irons are very hot and heavy; avoid ironing when small children are near, and never leave a hot iron unattended.

155

Iron a Shirt

Even so-called no-iron shirts often require ironing – but if you learn to do it yourself, you'll save enough on laundry bills to buy several more.

◉ Steps

1 Locate the label on your shirt that indicates the materials that were used in the garment.

2 Plug in the iron and set the dial to the recommended setting for that fabric. Linen and 100 per cent cotton take a high setting; wools and cotton blends call for medium heat; polyester, rayon, nylon, silk, acetate and acrylic all require a low heat setting.

Business Manners

3   Fill the iron with distilled (de-ionised) water if you will be using the steam setting on cotton or linen.

4   Test the iron on a small area to make sure you don't have the setting too high – this can damage or discolour the fabric.

5   Iron the back of the collar first, then the front, taking care to iron in from the edges a little at a time to avoid creases.

6   Open the cuffs fully. Iron inside first, then outside.

7   Iron the sleeves after smoothing them flat to avoid creases. Do the sleeve backs first, the fronts second.

8   Hang the shirt over the board so that you can extend one front panel of the shirt flat (with the collar at the narrower end of the board). Iron from shoulder to shirt-tail.

9   Rotate the shirt over the board so that you iron the back next, and the other front panel last.

✳ Tips

Hang your warm shirt on a hanger immediately to avoid rewrinkling it.

If you'll be wearing a buttoned jacket all day and are short of time, you need only iron the collar, sleeves and top of the front. If you'll be wearing a jumper all day, iron only the collar.

⚠ Warning

Irons are very hot and heavy; avoid ironing when small children are near, and never leave a hot iron unattended.

156
Shine Shoes

Want to keep your shoes looking as good as new? Learn how to shine them like a pro.

◎ Steps

1   Clean dust and dirt from the surface of your shoes or boots with a shoeshine brush or damp cloth.

Office Life

2   Select a wax or cream shoe polish that matches the leather's colour.

3   Use a shoe-polish brush (a small, soft brush that's distinct from the large, bristly shoeshine brush) to apply a conservative amount of polish to the surface of the leather. Brush in circular motions until the leather has a dull coating. Get into tight spots using an old soft-bristled toothbrush.

4   Wait up to 15 minutes, or until the polish completely or nearly dries, depending on the instructions for the polish.

5   Brush the shoes or boots with a shoeshine brush.

6   Buff them to a gleaming shine with a clean cotton cloth, such as an old sock or T-shirt.

 Tips

Don't polish suede or patent leather.

"Instant" shoe polishes generally do not last and can harm shoe leather.

Don't attempt to change the colour of leather with polish. Have a shoemaker dye the shoes.

157

Choose a Good Seat on an Aeroplane

Where should you sit on an aeroplane if you're prone to motion sickness? If you have a connecting flight? If you're travelling with kids? Ask an airline agent about reserving the right seat for you.

⊚ **Steps**

1   Request bulkhead seats – those behind the dividing walls of a plane – or a seat by one of the emergency exits if you want more leg room.

2   Choose an aisle seat for easier access to the overhead storage compartment and lavatories, as well as for faster disembarking.

3   Consider sitting near the lavatories if you are travelling with children.

4   Opt for the back of the plane if you want to spread out; there are usually fewer people in the back.

Business Travel

5   Sit towards the front if you want to get off the plane faster, which could be important if you're trying to make a tight connection. The front of the plane also tends to be a quieter ride.

6   Choose a seat toward the wings, which are the stability point for the plane, if motion sickness is a potential problem.

7   Sit near the galleys if you want early snack, drink or meal service.

✳ Tips

If you're travelling with a companion, reserve the aisle and window seat of a three-seat row. Because middle seats are the last to be sold, you have a good chance of having an extra seat.

Join a frequent-flier programme to increase your chances of getting a good seat on the plane.

⚠ Warning

Exit-door seats must be filled by passengers willing and able to help people in an emergency and may not be available for reservation. Check with your airline agent.

158

Exchange Currency

When you're travelling abroad, banks and legal money changers offer the best rates when you need to exchange one currency for another.

◎ Steps

1   Look in the business section of the local newspaper for the current exchange rates.

2   Find a legal money changer (a well-known bureau de change or an American Express Travel Service, for example) or bank, which offers better rates than an airport or hotel. If you withdraw money from an ATM, you'll receive the bank's exchange rate, but may incur transaction fees.

3   Show the cashier your passport.

4 Use your own calculator to ensure the accuracy of the exchange.

5 Sign the release form.

6 Count the money before you leave the desk, and take your time.

7 Get a receipt. Customs officials won't ask to see it, but it's always a good insurance policy to have one when you've exchanged money.

✳ Tips

Exchange a small amount of money before you leave for your trip. Exchange rates at the airport where you're going may be OK, but it's best to have a choice.

When you use traveller's cheques, a commission is taken out per cheque. Exchange larger denominations when possible.

Money changers don't exchange coins, so spend your loose change before you return.

Things You'll Need

❏ calculator

❏ passport

159

Make the Most of Your Frequent-Flier Miles

Flying can earn you frequent-flier miles, as can putting purchases on a credit card with an airline tie-in. After all that spending, don't waste those precious miles – learn the tricks for using them.

◉ Steps

1 Choose one frequent-flier programme and concentrate on maximising your benefits within that programme.

2 Know and use the frequent-flier programme's partners, who may range from florists to telephone companies to hotels.

3   Consult the programme's newsletter frequently for updates on new partners and promotions. If you don't receive the newsletter by post, call and request a subscription, or check online for newsletter postings.

4   Keep track of your miles. Work towards attaining elite status if you are a high-frequency traveller, or a free trip if you are a leisure traveller.

5   Save your free miles for flights that are usually expensive.

6   Check your statements carefully, and keep your travel receipts in case the airline forgets to credit your account properly.

✸ Tip

Purchase tickets using frequent-flier miles as early as possible – even a year in advance if you can. These tickets get snapped up quickly.

160

Make a Hotel Reservation

Comfortable and convenient places to stay – whether in a large hotel or a small bed-and-breakfast – will make your trip more pleasant. Here's how to arrange them without using a travel agent.

◉ Steps

1   Buy a travel guide to your destination, especially if you're not familiar with the area. Read up on accommodation options and areas where places to stay are plentiful.

2   Plan your arrival and departure dates. If possible, choose off-season dates when you may be able to save money on accommodation.

3   Choose the area you want to stay in. This generally depends on where you will be doing business or on the recreational or cultural sights you want to see.

4   Find two or three hotels in your price range that appeal to you.

5   Call each hotel. Tell them the dates you will be lodging there and your room requirements, and ask for the room rate. Ask about family

packages where kids stay for free or at a substantial discount, and about special deals that give you a discount on surrounding attractions.

6   Find out what other services are included in the room rate. Is a hot breakfast included? Afternoon tea?

7   Ask about any special rates that are available. For example, if you stay 4 nights during the low season, are you entitled to a special long weekend rate? If you adjust your dates slightly, can you get a better deal? Be sure the adjustment will be reflected in the final room rate.

8   Compare room rates and services and book one of the hotels. Be sure to specify a smoking or non-smoking room.

9   Reserve the room with your credit card. This will generally hold the room for you no matter what time you arrive.

✱ Tips

You can also request a guide to places to stay from the tourist office of the area you'll be visiting. Remember, though, that you may get more honest appraisals from an independent guidebook, from friends' recommendations or from various websites.

If you are arriving at a local airport, ask if the hotel provides free transport from the airport to the hotel.

Ask about other extras that may be important to you: fridge, hair dryer, iron, gym, on-site restaurant, swimming pool, video, film rental, wheelchair access, pet-friendly facilities.

⚠ Warning

Check the hotel's cancellation policy. These differ from hotel to hotel, but if you cancel without letting the hotel know within the specified time, you may have to pay for a night's accommodation.

161

Get a Hotel-Room Upgrade

Sometimes upgrading your hotel room is possible, and sometimes it's not. Your chances depend on a combination of the available space, your arrival time and luck.

1 Establish loyalty by always choosing the same hotel in cities you visit often. Being friendly with the reception staff never hurts.

2 Ask about freebies and other special deals when you book your reservation. If you don't ask, you usually don't get.

3 Join frequent-visitor programmes at the chain hotels you visit. Your points earn upgrades and free stays along with other perks.

4 Organise reunions, meetings or conferences at your favourite hotel. Lots of hotels say thanks with credit for upgrades or free nights, either at the time of the event or at a later date.

5 Trade airline frequent-flier points for upgrades at participating hotels. But weigh this option carefully – it's rarely the most cost-effective way to spend frequent-flier points.

6 Be vocal. If the room you were assigned isn't satisfactory – dirty, noisy or lacking the view you were promised – ask for an upgrade.

7 Offer to be appeased. If the staff makes a mistake that causes a delay or distress – say they misplace your luggage or, in a worst-case scenario, fail to make your room safe – make it known that an upgrade will help you forget all about the bad experience.

8 Take a chance on luck. Once in a while, you'll be in the right place at the right time. Budget rooms sometimes get overbooked, and the lucky guest who gets bumped up to the executive floor could turn out to be you.

✱ **Tip**

Friendliness and charm may help encourage a hotel receptionist to go the extra mile for you.

162

Prevent Jet Lag

Jet lag doesn't have to ruin the first few days of your trip abroad. A few simple tips will help keep it in check.

Travel

⊙ Steps

1 Start shifting your sleep-wake cycle to match that of your destination several days before departure, changing at the rate of one hour per day.

2 Begin adjusting to the time zone of your destination by resetting your watch at the beginning of your flight.

3 Sleep on the plane when it is night-time at your destination. Earplugs, headphones and an eye mask can help diminish noise and light.

4 Stay awake on the plane when it is daytime at your destination. Read a thriller with the light on and the window shade open, or walk around.

5 Drink plenty of water. The air on planes is extremely dry, and dehydration can worsen the effects of jet lag.

6 Avoid alcohol and caffeine while flying. They increase dehydration.

7 Exercise as much as you can on the flight during waking hours: stretch, walk down the aisles and do leg lifts (see 165 "Exercise on a Plane").

Things You'll Need

❑ earplugs

❑ headphones

❑ eye mask

163

Treat Jet Lag

Flying across numerous time zones can affect travellers for days. Try the following tips to speed up the adjustment process.

⊙ Steps

Daytime Arrival

1 Reset your watch to local time if you haven't done so already.

2   Eat a protein-packed breakfast, such as an omelette, which will help you stay awake.

3   Soak up natural sunlight to cue your body that it is time to be awake. Or spend your first day in well-lit places.

4   Get some exercise, but don't overdo it; a good option is a gentle walk outside during the day to get fresh air and keep your body moving.

5   Take a short nap if you are really weary, but do so before 2 pm and sleep for no longer than an hour.

6   Go to bed at a reasonable time. Even if you feel like dropping off at 5 pm, try to hold out until at least 8 or 9 pm so that you won't wake up too early the next morning.

Nighttime Arrival

1   Eat a high-carbohydrate meal, such as pasta, to help make you drowsy.

2   Plan to go to bed at the local bedtime, even if you aren't sleepy.

3   Think about other ways to induce sleep: a hot bath with lavender oil, a cup of chamomile tea or a massage. Keep lights dim.

4   Avoid sleeping late, even if you did not sleep well.

Tip

Make sure your hotel room is not too hot. You'll get the best night's sleep in a cool (but not cold) room.

⚠ Warnings

Avoid drinking alcohol to help you sleep. It will interfere with your body's natural sleep patterns. Also avoid drinking a lot of caffeinated drinks to keep yourself awake during the day. These will dehydrate you and make you more tired when they wear off.

Avoid driving, especially in an unfamiliar place, if you are overtired. If you must drive while weary, be very careful. Keep the window open and make frequent stops to keep sleepiness at bay.

Travel

Kill Time in an Airport

Waiting long hours at an airport can be boring and frustrating. Why not improve your mood by seeking out the attractions the airport has to offer?

⊙ Steps

1 Dissolve stress and increase energy by exercising in the airport gym. A growing number of airports now contain workout areas.

2 Power-walk around the entire airport if there is no gym. Store luggage in terminal lockers, lace up the walking shoes and get the blood pumping.

3 Surf the internet and answer e-mail at an internet kiosk to make the time fly. Keep in mind that you'll be charged for the time you spend online.

4 Purchase souvenirs and presents for friends and family at the airport's gift shops and retail outlets.

5 Get your shoes polished. Many larger airports feature shine specialists to buff and polish your shoes.

6 Enjoy a drink in the airport bar if there is one. In some airports the day's big sporting event will probably be blaring on the television.

7 Bring a good book or a stack of your favourite magazines. Airport time can constitute some of the most peaceful reading time you will ever get.

⚠ Warning

Keep your eye on a clock at all times, and check the departure screens regularly to ensure that you do not miss your flight.

Exercise on a Plane

Combat poor circulation, swelling, sore joints and lethargy on cramped flights by doing a short exercise routine. At the very least, you'll entertain your fellow passengers.

⊙ Steps

1 Squeeze a tennis ball, a squash ball or even a pair of socks with your hands until they're tired.

2 Keep the balls of your feet planted and raise your legs using your calf muscles. If this is too easy, place your hand luggage on your knees. Continue until tired.

3 Plant your heels firmly and raise your toes as high as possible. Hold for five seconds, and relax. Repeat until tired.

4 Place your hands on your armrests and raise your knees slowly (together is harder than one at a time) towards your chin. Lower them slowly. Repeat until tired.

5 Cross your legs. Rotate the dangling foot in as wide a circle as possible. Continue until tired.

6 Stretch your neck by keeping your chin close to your throat and tilting your head forwards. Roll your head from one shoulder to the other, but avoid rotating it backwards.

7 Flex your trapezius muscles by doing shoulder hunches. Lower your shoulders, and then raise them up towards your ears into a shrug. Hold for five seconds. Continue until tired.

8 Arch your torso gently backwards and forwards like a cat.

9 Flex your gluteus muscles and hold for as long as possible. Squeezing your rear like this may occasion strange glances, but these muscles are the biggest in the human body and need to be exercised, too.

✱ Tip

When aisles are relatively empty and the seatbelt sign is off, walk around, stretch and do lunges. To lunge, take a big step (about half your height) and gently lower yourself as far as you can while keeping the torso upright and back leg straight. Return to a standing position by stepping either forward with the rear foot or backward with the front foot. Repeat. Once you become skilled, you'll be able to work up a sweat (and an audience) lunging to the toilet and back.

166

Eat Healthily on a Plane

With a little foresight and know-how, you can actually get a healthy – and edible – meal in the sky.

◎ Steps

1   Call your airline at least 24 hours before you fly and order a special-diet meal at no extra cost. Vegetarian, Hindu, kosher, low-salt and sugar-free options are usually available. A special-diet meal doesn't guarantee that the food will be good, but at least you'll get some special preparation.

2   Pack a meal, if you have the time. Bring food that travels well and that requires no cutting, messiness or permanent containers. Steer clear of foods that will bother other passengers, such as items with too much crunch or odour.

3   Bring an energy bar or some other meal replacement in case the in-flight meal is inedible or your flight is delayed.

4   Eat in the airport if you don't want to entrust your airline with your culinary fate. Large airports have the usual variety of fast-food franchises, so pick what you know to be the most nourishing.

5   Follow any alcohol or caffeine consumption with plenty of water to avoid becoming dehydrated.

✱ Tip

Culinary possibilities open up on long international flights with major carriers. Call in advance and ask what special meals are available – you may be pleasantly surprised.

⚠ Warnings

Avoiding MSG (monosodium glutamate) is tricky. You can speak to your

Business Travel

airline, but don't expect a promise that MSG will be absent from your food. Consider bringing your own meal if you are sensitive to MSG.

Be wary of vegetarian breakfasts if you want something filling – you might get just a banana or juice.

167
Sleep on a Plane

Sleeping through the night or even taking a power nap on a plane can be tricky. But with the proper preparations, a satisfactory snooze is possible for almost everyone.

⊙ Steps

1 Reserve your seat in advance. Window seats give you a wall to lean on, and your neighbour won't need to disturb you on the way to the toilet.

2 Buy and pack in your hand luggage the following: travel pillow and eye mask, earplugs, comfortable clothing, slippers and bottled water.

3 Make sure that your body will be tired for the flight: before your departure avoid sleeping in, napping or consuming caffeine, and try to get some exercise.

4 Grab a pillow and blanket as soon as you get on the plane. Remember, your seat is reserved, but blankets may not be.

5 Scan the cabin for better seats once the flight is under way. A row of empty seats with movable armrests is the best situation for sleeping on a plane – aside from first class.

6 Adjust your seat for maximum comfort. If you can't put it back far enough, try putting a pillow or blanket behind your lower back to make you more reclined.

7 Ask what time the in-flight meal will be served. Falling asleep is easier on a full stomach.

8 Tell your neighbour that you plan to sleep. The purpose is twofold: he or she will leave you alone, and can discourage the flight attendants from disturbing you while you sleep.

Travel

Tip

Most travel shops carry a variety of pillows designed for sleeping in an upright position. Budget travellers find the inflatable U-shaped vinyl pillows satisfactory and compact.

⚠ **Warning**

Consult your doctor before taking any variety of sleeping pill.

Things You'll Need

☐ travel pillow

☐ eye mask

☐ earplugs

☐ bottled water

168

↟ ↟ ↟

Learn Key Foreign Phrases Without a Phrase Book

You don't need a phrase book to learn a few key words in the local language where you're travelling. A little effort will make your travel easier and your hosts feel appreciated.

⊙ **Steps**

1   Set a reasonable goal about what you would like to learn, and stick with it. This can be as simple as learning a few basic greetings, polite terms of address, or how to order your favourite dish in a restaurant.

2   Pay attention to how others greet one another or part from one another; learning proper greetings and goodbyes will always engender goodwill.

3   Find yourself a few good "teachers" – a hotel receptionist, a waiter in a restaurant, a taxi driver. This doesn't have to be someone you will spend a great deal of time with, just someone who appreciates your curiosity about the language and with whom you can comfortably interact about day-to-day needs.

4   Ask how to say a few words that will help introduce you to the language's sounds. You don't need a common language to do this; pointing and gesturing will do just fine. Learning how to say your teacher's name, the name of the town you're visiting, or the numbers one to five is a good place to start.

5   Jot down words as you learn them, making up your own phonetic system that will help you remember how they sound. Have your teacher pronounce the word while you write it down the way you think it sounds.

6   Repeat new words or phrases to your teacher immediately after she says them. Ask her to say the word again. Repeat it, making adjustments in your pronunciation as you notice differences.

7   Keep a running list of new words, and review it several times throughout the day. The key to learning vocabulary in a foreign language is review.

8   Try using your new words or phrases with locals other than your teacher. Ask them to repeat the words you have learned, so you can get used to hearing the ways other people pronounce them.

 Tip

Keep your sense of humour. Trying to speak a foreign language often feels silly, embarrassing or frustrating at first, but be persistent – the payoff is worth it.

✓ 169 Tip for Service When Travelling

Tipping is de rigueur in most of the world, but the methods and percentages vary. In some countries, a service charge is added to restaurant or hotel bills in lieu of gratuities. In many others, waiting staff rely on tips to bring their wage up to a decent level. The following are suggested guidelines only. Consult an up-to-date travel guide for more information about local customs.

COUNTRY	SUGGESTED TIP	NOTES
Australia	Optional	Tipping is not usual in Australia, but a small tip for good service by waiters, hotel porters and taxi drivers is appreciated.
Canada	10–20%	Tipping is usual and expected in restaurants and bars, for taxis and for food delivery.
China	None	Tipping is not usual in China.
Egypt	Variable	Tips are expected by waiters, hotel staff, tour guides, drivers (but not taxi drivers).Tip generously if you have had good service.
France	15–20%	The 15% service charge is usually included in the price in restaurants. Many people leave another 5% or so on top.
Germany	Variable	Service charge is included in restaurant bills but small tips on top are appreciated. Give taxi drivers a 10% tip.
Hong Kong	10–15%	Most restaurants add about 10% to a bill and you are expected to add another 5% or so on top.

COUNTRY	SUGGESTED TIP	NOTES
India	Variable	About 10% is added to the bill in tourist hotels and restaurants. Drivers and tour guides will expect a tip; if they have been especially helpful or spent a long time with you, tip generously.
Ireland	10–12.5%	Tipping is usual in restaurants and for taxis, but not in hotels. Restaurants sometimes include a service charge in the bill.
Italy	Up to 15%	Service of 15% is sometimes included in restaurant bills. If not, leave a tip of 10% or so. Some family restaurants do not expect a tip. Tip taxi drivers and hotel porters if they have been helpful.
Japan	None	Service charges are included in restaurant and hotel bills; tipping is not necessary and may even cause offence.
Mexico	Variable	Expected by taxi drivers, waiters, food delivery services and hotel staff.
New Zealand	Optional	Tipping is not usual in New Zealand, but is becoming more common in larger cities where you can tip 5–10% of a restaurant bill.
Thailand	Optional	Not usual except in upmarket hotels.
United Kingdom	10–15%	Usual for restaurants, although some include service in the bill, especially for larger parties. Taxi drivers expect a similar tip.
United States	15–20%	Essential for waiters and cocktail waiters, taxi drivers and hotel room service. Also tip a couple of dollars to hotel maids and bellhops.

Business travel

Make Small Talk

Small talk can be a big challenge, but preparation and confidence are all you really need.

Steps

1 Practise. Converse with everyone you encounter: cashiers, waiters, people you're in a queue with, neighbours, co-workers, and kids. Chat with people unlike yourself, from the elderly to teenagers to tourists.

2 Read everything: cookbooks, newspapers, magazines, reviews, product inserts, maps, signs and catalogues. Everything is a source of information that can be turned into interesting conversations.

3 Force yourself to get into small-talk situations, such as doctors' waiting rooms, cocktail parties, and meetings at the office. Accept invitations or host your own gathering.

4 Immerse yourself in culture, both high and low. Television, music, sports, fashion, art and poetry are great sources of chat. If you can't stand Shakespeare, your dislike of the bard is also a good topic for discussion.

5 Keep a diary. Write down funny stories you hear, beautiful things you see, quotes, observations, shopping lists, and phone calls you made. That story about the time when the operator at the call centre misunderstood you could become an opening line.

6 Talk to yourself in the mirror. Make a random list of topics and see what you have to say on the subjects. Tennis, Russia, butter, hip-hop, shoes – the more varied your list, the better.

7 Expand your horizons. Go home a new way. Try sushi. Play pinball. Go online. Paint a watercolour. Bake a pie. Try something new every day.

8 Be a better listener. Did your boss say that she suffers from migraines? Has your doctor just had twins? These are opportunities for making small talk.

9 Work on building up your confidence, overcoming shyness and banishing any feelings of stage fright. Remember, the more you know, the more you know you can talk about.

Office Party

171

Survive the Party

You agreed to go to the office party. Instead of dwelling on how you allowed such a thing to happen, have fun by following these simple tips.

⊙ Steps

1 Enjoy yourself, first and foremost. Would you rather be at home washing the dishes? If the answer is yes, keep thinking of mundane chores until you find one you would not want to be doing at the moment.

2 You see someone you think you'd like to know better. He or she ignores you. So? Pat yourself on the back for knowing that your soul mate is not necessarily hanging out in a meat market. Let it go and find someone else with better manners.

3 Be someone you're not – try on a new hat. Play the part of the spoiled rich girl, the alpha-wolf guy, the dumb blonde.

4 Be careful not to drink too much, in case you are approached by someone with a bad pick-up line. "May I end this sentence with a proposition?" might work on you if you have had a few too many.

5 Remember, though, that as lame as pick-up lines might be, the person is making an effort to show an interest in you. If you are even remotely interested, laugh, say hello and begin a normal conversation.

Office Party

6 Be polite if someone wants to talk to you and you aren't interested. If the person won't leave you alone, say that you have a boyfriend or girlfriend.

7 Save your flirting for when you really want to use it.

✳ Tips

Be sure you know how you're getting home before you go out.

Interestingly enough, 71 per cent of men report success when they use the pickup line "Hi".

⚠ Warning

Don't put yourself into a dangerous situation, such as being alone in a dark alley with a strange man – or woman.

172

Flirt

Not a natural flirt? Don't worry – anyone can learn the basic social skills that will attract others.

⊙ Steps

1 Be confident – it's the magical charm that makes others want to get to know you.

2 Smile, smile, smile.

3 Think playful thoughts when gearing up to flirt. Flirts are fun and engaging, and they love to play with others.

4 Compliment a stranger or acquaintance on his or her clothes, eyes, smile or sense of humour, for starters.

5 Keep your body language open and inviting: make eye contact, lightly touch the person's hand or arm when telling a story, toss your head back when you laugh.

6 Initiate stimulating conversation. At a loss for words? Ask open-ended questions about the flirtee's job, home town, family, recent films seen or thoughts about a painting on the wall.

7   Open up about yourself, giving someone even more reason to like you. But don't go on and on – the goal is to engage and intrigue, not bore.

8   Gauge the person's interest carefully. If you sense a red light – or worse, smug ridicule – make your exit graciously and immediately. You've got nicer people to meet.

9   Progress in your flirtation, paying attention to cues from the object of your interest. If you perceive a sensual or sexual connection, make a bold move – ask for a date.

✳ Tips

Avoid negative body language, such as crossing your arms, scowling, appearing overly stressed, looking downwards or walking in a hurry when you don't really need to.

Give yourself time to learn the types of conversation starters that work for you. Practise flirting wherever you can – at the local shop or launderette, or with your friends.

⚠ Warning

Sexually suggestive remarks or touching is inappropriate among colleagues. Keep any office flirting innocent at all times.

173
Tango

Born in the brothels of Argentina, the tango is synonymous with passion. Although the dance is relatively free-form, you can do a lot with two basic moves: the walking step and the rock step.

⊙ Steps

1   Face your partner and stand closer together than you would in most other ballroom dances – close enough for your torsos to touch.

2   If you're the leader, place your right hand on the middle of your partner's lower back. Extend your left hand out to your side with your arm bent and grasp your partner's right hand in a loose grip. Your

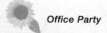

partner should place her left hand on your right shoulder and place her right hand lightly in your palm with her right elbow bent.

3 On the first beat, walk forwards slowly with your left foot, placing down your heel first and then your toes. Your partner will mirror each of your movements on every beat throughout the dance – in this case, moving her right foot backwards, landing her toes and then her heel.

4 On the second beat, step forwards slowly with your right foot so that it moves past your left. You should feel as if you are slinking forwards.

5 On the third beat, step forwards quickly with your left foot, then immediately slide your right foot quickly to the right side and shift your weight to that foot.

6 On the fourth beat, bring your left foot slowly to your right, leaving your left leg slightly bent as your feet come together. Your weight should still be on your right foot.

7 Now, shift your weight to your left foot and do a right forwards rock step: While making a half-turn clockwise, step forwards quickly on your right foot, and then quickly shift your weight back to your left foot. With your right foot, slowly step forwards to complete the half turn.

8 Bring your foot together, bring your left foot up next to your right and repeat steps 3 to 7.

✳ Tips

Bear in mind that your feet barely leave the floor as you dance.

This isn't a subtle way to meet people.

174

Salsa

Listen to the rhythm of the music as you learn this popular Latin dance. You can learn the basic salsa steps in less than an hour, and sashay all over the dance floor before you know it.

Office Party

◎ Steps

1   Get in position by facing your partner. If you are the leader, place your right hand on your partner's waist, slightly around the back. Extend your left arm diagonally to chest height with your elbow bent at a right angle and your palm raised. Grasp your partner's right hand in a loose grip; your partner's left hand should be on your right shoulder.

2   On the first beat, step forwards with your left foot. Your partner will mirror each of your movements throughout the dance; for example, on the first beat she will step backwards with her right foot.

3   Step in place with your right foot on the second beat.

4   Step back with your left foot on the third beat so that you are back in the starting position, and hold in place for the fourth beat.

5   Step back with your right foot on the fifth beat.

6   Step in place with your left foot on the sixth beat.

7   Step forwards with your right foot on the seventh beat so that you are back in the starting position, and hold for the eighth beat.

8   Repeat, starting at step 2.

✳ Tips

You can add more complicated moves once you've grasped the basic salsa step.

Don't use exaggerated hip movement. That sexy swing will come naturally as you let yourself feel the rhythm.

Some salsa clubs offer free or inexpensive introductory classes or specials on certain nights of the week.

175
Jive

Modern jive is a dance style that evolved in the 1990s. It can be danced to many kinds of music, from rock'n'roll and swing to much of contemporary pop. There are hundreds of possible variations, but here is a basic move to get started.

Office Party

◉Steps

1 Get in position by facing your partner. If you are the leader (usually the man), turn your hands palm upwards in front of you at waist level. Your partner lays her hands lightly over yours.

2 Initiate the dance with a step backwards by both partners. Bend your fingers to create a grip and stretch your arms so that you can feel the tension of your two bodies pulling away from one another. Keep the handhold light – neither of you should grip with your thumbs.

3 Step together on the next beat, at the same time turning anti-clockwise through 90 degrees, so that you are side by side.

4 Both twist 180 degrees clockwise on the next beat so that you are again side by side but facing in the opposite direction.

5 Both twist 90 degrees anti-clockwise to face one another. If you are the leader, raise your left hand to shoulder height. The partner mirrors this by raising her right hand. Ensure the hands are palm to palm, touching but not holding.

6 If you are the leader, push downwards to propel the partner into a spin. The partner spins through 360 degrees and returns to face the leader.

7 Resume the light grip with both hands and both step back, once more creating tension in the arms as you pull apart. You are ready to repeat the move or try another variant.

✳Tips

Keep your arms at waist level most of the time. When pulling apart, don't extend your arms out fully straight – if you do, the effect is jerky and definitely uncool.

Some jive clubs offer inexpensive introductory classes on certain nights of the week. You will need lessons to pick up enough moves to make jiving worthwhile.

Office Party

Choose Champagne

Sparkling wine – called Champagne if it comes from the Champagne region of France – is made from Chardonnay, Pinot Noir, Muscat and other grape varieties.

⊙ Steps

1   Learn to look for the words "méthode champenoise" on the label. True Champagnes and the best sparkling wines from other regions are made by this process of double-fermentation – once in barrels or vats and a second time in bottles.

2   Learn the different types of sparkling wines, from extra-brut (the driest) to extra-sec (very dry), sec (dry), demi-sec and doux (sweet). The great vintage Champagnes are found in the brut category.

3   Taste various types of sparkling wine and Champagne to get an idea of what kinds appeal most to you. One way to do this is to check the wine seller's events calendars and attend Champagne tastings.

4   Ask friends whose taste you respect for advice and recommendations, and talk to wine sellers, too.

5   Learn the histories and winemaking styles of various sparkling wine houses in France, California and elsewhere. Remember that Germany, Spain and Italy also make sparkling wines.

✱ Tips

Sparkling wine terms can be confusing. "Brut," for example, is drier than "extra dry."

Only sparkling wines from the Champagne region of France are correctly called Champagnes – but the term is still casually used for all sparkling wines, especially in the United States. Some California sparkling wines will even say "Champagne" on the label.

Less expensive sparkling wines are usually made by the charmat bulk process, in which all the fermentation takes place in vats.

Office Party

Open a Champagne Bottle

It takes some skill to open a bottle of Champagne so that the bubbly ends up in the flutes and not all over your guests.

⦿ Steps

1 Remove the foil from the cork.

2 Angle the bottle away from everyone so that if the cork pops out, it won't injure anyone.

3 Untwist the wire restraint securing the cork.

4 Wrap the bottle's neck and cork in a clean napkin.

5 Take hold of the cork with the napkin and gently untwist.

6 Continue untwisting, or hold the cork in place and twist the bottle itself.

7 Slowly ease the cork out of the bottle's neck. Wait for a soft pop. Pour.

✱ Tips

Keep glasses nearby and ready to catch the foam.

To preserve and best appreciate the effervescence of any sparkling wine, use the tall, narrow glasses known as flutes. Old-fashioned wide Champagne glasses allegedly cause bubbles to dissipate quickly.

Read Your Date's Body Language

Body language says a lot about what someone is really thinking.

⦿ Steps

Positive Body Language

1 Notice if your date's posture is good yet relaxed. A slouched date probably isn't having a good time. A date who's sitting up is paying attention.

Office Party

2   Observe whether your date makes good eye contact. If he keeps looking into your eyes, you've got it made.

3   Is your date leaning forward? Then you aren't a stranger any more.

4   Be aware of any physical contact. Holding hands is a great sign.

5   Notice if your date has her palms up, which indicates a friendly warmth.

6   Know that your date is listening to you if he nods at appropriate times during the conversation; this indicates that your words are being heard.

7   Pay attention to whether your date is in sync with you and constantly reflecting your behaviour. Does she shift in her seat when you do? Does he pick up your speed and tone when he's speaking? This occurs unconsciously and indicates a good rhythm between you – it's not just a copycat game.

Negative Body Language

1   Take note if your date's arms are crossed. This suggests there's a wall between the two of you.

2   Beware if your date is yawning. This is a bad sign – unless it's because she was up all night thinking about you.

3   Notice if your date is nodding at inappropriate times or seems to be nodding constantly during your conversation. Your date may be thinking about something else.

4   Is your date looking at everything but you? Be worried.

5   Notice if your date is keeping some distance between you. Personal space is one thing, but if your date is not standing next to you when you're waiting in a cinema queue together, that's a bad sign.

✱ Tip

Interpreting body language isn't cut-and-dried; allow for the fact that your interpretation may be wrong.

⚠ Warning

Avoid pointing out your date's body language to him or her – this may put your date on the defensive.

Office Party

Kiss on a Date

The date's gone well, and now it's almost over. Here are some tips on the how and when of kissing.

⊙ Steps

1 Look for positive body language, such as eye contact, uncrossed arms and head tilted towards you.

2 Do it. Waiting just makes the moment awkward.

3 Maintain eye contact as you close in. Try not to close your eyes until after making lip contact.

4 Tilt your head slightly to one side to avoid bumping noses.

5 Press your lips gently against your date's. Try not to suck his or her breath away just yet.

6 Release. Look into your date's eyes. If he or she isn't looking back at you the same way, then you probably shouldn't continue.

7 Kiss your date again. There's more flexibility to this kiss.

8 Explore – softly kiss your date's neck, ears and eyelashes. By this time, you'll have a better feel for how and where to kiss your date.

✳ Tip

Keep the kissing simple for now. Use a soft touch that will calm your date, especially if this kiss is the first one.

Avoid a Hangover

The best way to avoid a hangover, of course, is never to drink at all. But if abstinence is not a part of your plans, check out these proven techniques.

⊙ Steps

1 Eat before you drink. Starchy carbohydrates such as bread and pasta will slow the absorption of alcohol.

2 Avoid very sweet drinks that disguise their alcohol content, and avoid mixing different types of alcohol.

3 Drink water in between alcoholic drinks to prevent dehydration.

4 Eat hearty food while you are drinking.

5 Drink a few glasses of water when you get home.

✱ Tip

If you get a really bad hangover, keep track of what you had to drink the night before and avoid it next time.

⚠ Warning

Avoid aspirin or ibuprofen if you have stomach ulcers or gastritis.

181

Care for a Hangover

The headache, nausea, thirst and fatigue you feel are all symptoms of dehydration. Follow these steps to eliminate those symptoms and get back to feeling your best.

⊙ Steps

1 Drink water as soon as you get up in the morning to rehydrate yourself. If possible, have a sports drink. The electrolytes and nutrients in a sports drink can replenish your body's depleted reserves.

2 Drink even more water if you plan to have coffee. Caffeine is a mild diuretic and can contribute to dehydration.

3 Stick to liquids that are at room temperature. Drinks that are excessively hot or cold will be even more of a shock to your struggling stomach.

4 Take an over-the-counter pain reliever such as aspirin or ibuprofen to relieve a pounding headache or body aches.

Office Party

5　Eat easily digestible foods when you're ready. Fresh fruit, toast and
water-based soups are all easy on the stomach. Harder-to-digest
foods, such as eggs and milk, can cause stomach problems.

6　Relax, rest or go back to bed. Allow some time for your body to feel
positive effects from your treatments.

✳ Tip

Take preventative measures beforehand: drink responsibly and in
moderation. If you've drunk in excess and suspect you'll be hung over
the next morning, drink a few glasses of water just before you go to bed.

⚠ Warnings

Do not take a paracetamol-based painkiller to relieve symptoms.
Combining paracetamol and alcohol can damage your liver. Consider
ibuprofen instead.

If you are an excessive drinker, use caution when taking any over-the-
counter painkillers.

182

Fill in Your Tax Return

If you are a self-assessed income tax payer you – or your
accountant acting on your behalf – must fill in your annual
income tax return. This provides the figures on which you pay
your income tax.

◎ Steps

1　Make sure that you have a copy of the Inland Revenue guide SA150,
"How To Fill in Your Tax Return" (it should have been included with
your blank tax return). This tells you how to complete every box in
the form.

2　Begin by completing pages 2 and 3 of the form. This will tell you
whether you need to acquire and supplementary pages. These can be
ordered from the Inland Revenue web pages (inlandrevenue.gov.uk).

3   If you send your completed tax return in by the end of September, the Inland Revenue will calculate the tax payable for you. Otherwise, forms (with calculations) must be returned by the end of the following January – failure will result in a £100 fine.

4   Gather together all of the financial information you need to fill in your tax return. This will include payslips and your P60 if you are an employee, or a copy of your accounts if you are self-employed or a partner. Don't send invoices and bank statements with your tax form – keep them safe in case they are required for inspection.

5   Taking a blue or black pen, work through the tax return filling in the boxes clearly when required. Unless otherwise requested, enter all figures numerically. Don't include pence – round the values down to the nearest pound.

6   Complete any supplementary pages that may be needed. Sign and date the form and return it to the Inland Revenue in the envelope provided. Don't send any documents or cheques with your tax return – requests for payment will be made soon enough!

✳ Tips

You don't have to wait until the end of September/January deadlines to file your tax returns. Get them out of the way as soon as you can – it's one less thing to worry about.

You can also choose to fill in your tax return online. Look on the Inland Revenue's web pages: www.inlandrevenue.gov.uk.

183

Claim Tax Credits

Nine out of ten families with children are entitled to tax credits. But you don't need to have children to qualify. Here's how you can find out how to claim your entitlements.

◎ Steps

1   There are two different types of tax credit: Child Tax Credit and Working Tax Credit.

2   You can get tax credits if you are responsible for a child, or if you work but have a low income. By answering a few simple questions you can

find out which tax credits you are entitled to and the amount you could get.

3   Look at the Inland Revenue's Tax Credits web pages. This has an online questionnaire which will automatically assess your entitlement and enable you to apply online (taxcredits.inlandrevenue.gov.uk).

4   To answer the entitlement questions you may need the following details: payslips or P60 and National Insurance number; if self-employed, your accounts and unique tax reference number (UTR); details of any Social Security benefits you and/or your partner received during the previous tax year; Child Benefit details; approved childcare provider's information; bank details; other income for the previous tax year, such as, income from savings or pensions.

✳ Tips

Families with combined incomes of up to £58,000 can claim child tax credits, while families earning up to £66,000 will receive some help during the first year of a child's life – it will be paid on top of the universal child benefit that all parents receive, regardless of their income.

The government says all families with one child and an income of under £13,000 a year will be guaranteed a total of £54.25 a week from April 2003.

184

Determine the Type of Life Insurance You Need

The best life insurance to have is the kind that is in force when you die. But since most of us live a long time, some thought should go into the type of contract we choose.

⊙ Steps

1   Determine how long you want your life insurance coverage to be in effect – for example, from now until your children finish college, your partner retires from work, or throughout your entire life.

2   Buy a term (fixed-length) contract with an increasing premium if that length of time is less than four years.

Savings

3   Buy a term contract with a level premium if you need coverage for a
    longer time (5, 10, 15 or 20 years).

4   Buy a permanent contract if you wish to provide a death benefit for
    your beneficiary no matter how long you live.

 Tips

Most types of permanent insurance (often called whole-life) have a cash
value. You may be able to borrow against it at a low interest rate while
keeping most of the death benefit in force.

If your employer offers term life insurance and that's what you need, buy
all you can because group life is the least expensive term insurance
available.

185
Exploit Tax-Free Savings Opportunities

In most cases, interest you make from a savings account will
be subject to tax – this will usually be deducted by the bank
or building society. Here are some ways in which you can
save without paying tax.

⊙ **Steps**

1   Anyone over the age of 16 is allowed to put cash into an Individual
    Savings Account (ISA). These are tax-protective "wrappers" for your
    money. Over the course of a tax year you can invest up to £3,000 into
    a cash mini ISA or you can put up to £3,000 into the cash component
    of a maxi ISA.

2   Besides being tax-free, many cash ISAs also pay excellent rates of
    interest compared with other savings products. (To make the best use
    of your cash ISA allowance, use it for money you don't expect to need
    in the near future – that way you don't lose the tax-free benefit.)

3   Monitor the rates paid by other cash ISAs – you are entitled to switch
    your ISA to another provider if they offer a more competitive rate of
    interest. A brief review of competing rates every few months should
    do the trick.

4 If you're a non-taxpayer then you shouldn't pay any tax on your savings. Banks and building societies are required to deduct tax from the interest they pay you unless you first fill out a form – officially known as an "R85" – confirming that you are a legitimate non-taxpayer. The interest on your savings is then paid to you in full.

 Tips

If you have a spouse who's a non-taxpayer, then open an account in their name and get them to fill in Form R85.

Whether we like it or not, most of us don't expect to have to work beyond the standard retirement age: we expect *some* sort of mechanism to be in place to care for us – after all, we've spent all of our working lives contributing taxes for just this time, haven't we? Think again! With life expectancy in the UK ever on the increase it's going to be increasingly difficult to fund the traditional "old-age" pension. And the word from the experts is stark: the vast majority of us are not investing anything like sufficiently for that time. Although the pension route is the most common, it's only one of a number of approaches to saving for retirement.

PENSION PLANS

A pension is an income that you receive when you retire. To build up a big enough pot to provide that income, there must first have been some serious saving going on. To encourage us to this end, the Government provides concessions, chipping in the tax that you have paid (or would pay) on that money you've saved. These contributions form a pension fund, which is invested over the years until your retirement. Pension plans take many different forms. Company schemes are usually good value for money since the employer also makes monthly contributions. "Final salary" schemes, in which the pension is based on your income at the time of retirement, are now increasingly hard to find: the occupational schemes in public services such as the police, fire, civil service and teaching professions are just about the best on offer anywhere. Supported by the government, the new "stakeholder" pensions are also worth considering for medium- or high-income earners – and for the self-employed, who have traditionally received a very poor deal from pension schemes.

- ❑ Efficient way to save
- ❑ Stock market has traditionally provided the highest returns on investment
- ❑ Harder to succumb to temptation and spend the money before retirement
- ❑ Government contributes; employer contributes if in a company scheme
- ❑ Recent legislation makes it relatively easy to transfer between schemes

AGAINST:
- ❑ Charges higher and more complex than other investments
- ❑ Requires a degree of expertise (or at least an investment of time) to monitor progress
- ❑ Inflexible in respect to how you receive your pension money once you retire
- ❑ Not easy to estimate what your plan will be worth 10, 20, 30 or 40 years down the line

ALTERNATIVES TO PENSIONS

Pensions have have some bad press in recent years. And not without due cause. It's not very helpful trotting out the great stock-market mantra, "think in the long term", when a market fluctuation has just wiped off 25 per cent of the value of your pension a week before you were due to retire. Unsurprisingly, some have chosen to look away from traditional pension plans. For the cautious, there are some very safe options, such as the National Savings and Investments' guaranteed income or equity bonds. These provide a risk-free way of playing the stock market – even if the returns on offer are not earth-shattering. In recent times, a popular – yet in many ways just as risky – alternative has been investment in property. Buying-to-let offers a regular income and, if you buy in the right area, a phenomenal growth on the value of your original investment. But that only holds true during a property boom. And they don't last for ever.

Change Your Bank

Banks and building societies serve you, not the other way
around: if you're unhappy with your service here is what to do.

⊙ Steps

1   Complain in writing to your bank. Many banking features – such as
    account charges – are at the discretion of the management. You may
    be able to get a better deal without changing accounts.

2   Almost all British banks and building societies produce packs that
    enable you to change accounts and automatically transfer standing
    orders and Direct Debits. This entails little more than filling out a form.

3   Don't close your existing bank account until the new one is up and
    running to your satisfaction.

4   Request an immediate overdraft facility.

5   Contact your employer's payroll department to have your salary paid
    into the new account.

6   Check that automated payments in and out have been made. If there
    have been no problems after three months, contact your previous
    bank to close your old account.

✳ Tip

Make sure that you have enough "float" to cover both accounts during
the interim period when both are running concurrently.

Pay Monthly Bills on Time

Paying your bills promptly will help you avoid penalty fees and
interest charges. Follow these steps and keep your finances
in good order.

⊙ Steps

1 Set aside a special place to put your bills when they arrive, such as a desk, a special section in a drawer or a bill inbox. As soon as you receive them, open your bills, then put them in this place.

2 Set aside two times each month – two weeks apart – to pay your bills. The middle and end of the month are good times.

3 If possible, phone the companies that send you bills and ask them to revise your payment due dates to correspond with one of the two times you plan to pay your bills each month.

4 Mark your calendar to remind you of bill-paying dates and to help you keep to your schedule.

5 Pay your bills with cheques or money orders, then note the cheque number, the date and the amount paid on the receipt portion of each bill.

6 Even if these are not business expenses, it's a good idea to file away and keep invoices for a few years. (In business you should keep them for seven years.)

7 Place the envelopes containing your payments next to your keys so that you will remember to take them with you and mail them immediately.

✳ Tips

Some credit card companies, mortgage lenders and finance companies change due dates. Check the due dates for such bills when they arrive.

Utility and phone companies are usually a little more flexible and will wait for a few days before they send you a reminder notice.

Some companies may give a discount for bills paid either by standing order or Direct Debit.

For added efficiency, consider getting a bank account that allows you to arrange for bills to be paid automatically from your current account. You can kick off the payment buy making a phone call or from the internet.

Live Within Your Budget

Living within your budget can be challenging. A few simple practices can help ensure that you are successful.

◉ Steps

1 List all of your expenses, savings and income from the past year. Use your bank statement, credit card receipts and bills to do this. There are many computer-based financial programs that may help.

2 Determine, as accurately as possible, what expenses you expect to have over the next year. You can project expenses for a shorter period, such as the next three months, then multiply by four for yearly expenses.

3 Enter this information into a ledger or computer program (home finance software or as spreadsheet) to accurately track income and expenses.

4 Determine what you can reasonably afford to spend each month and then track how well you are doing by entering actual expenses into the ledger or computer program.

5 If you find that you are spending less than you had anticipated, you may want to put more money in your savings account to help out with unexpected expenses.

6 If you find that you are spending more than anticipated, try identifying the items you don't necessarily need (new clothes, CDs, eating out) and avoid purchasing them until you are back within your budget.

✱ Tips

Allocate a portion of your income for savings and retirement – for example, company, personal or stakeholder pension plans.

Consider setting aside up to 20 per cent of your take-home income for savings.

⚠ Warning

Avoid trying to forecast your expenses too far into the future. Doing so can result in inaccurate budgets and overspending.

Managing Your Money

Calculate Your Net Worth

Calculating your net worth is easy if the necessary information is readily available. Doing this will help you when deciding whether to make major purchases.

⊙ Steps

1 List all of your fixed assets, such as property and cars, at their current value.

2 List all of your liquid assets: cash, bank accounts, stocks and bonds.

3 List all jewellery, furniture and household items at their current value.

4 Add together all of the above. These are your total assets.

5 Subtract all of your debts, such as your mortgage, car loan and credit card balances, from your total assets. The result is your net worth.

6 Re-evaluate and update your net worth calculations on an annual basis.

✳ Tips

Be realistic when evaluating the current value of your assets. Such information can be useful in determining whether you are adequately insured. Share the information with your insurance company to help you decide.

Remember to use the net value (after-tax) of any stocks, shares and bonds when calculating their value.

Calculate Your Credit Standing

Lenders use your debt-to-income ratio – or how much you owe on credit cards and loans compared with how much you earn – to help evaluate your credit standing.

1 Add up your total net monthly income. This includes your monthly wages and any overtime, commissions or bonuses that are guaranteed; plus any other payments received, such as interest or maintenance payment. If your income varies, calculate the monthly average for the past two years. Include any additional income.

2 Add up your monthly debt obligations. This includes all of your credit card bills, loan and mortgage payments. Make sure to include your monthly rent payments if applicable.

3 Divide your total monthly debt obligations by your total monthly income. This is your total debt-to-income ratio.

4 If your ratio is higher than 0.36 – which industry professionals would call a score of 36 – you need to take action. The lower the score, the better. A figure higher than 36 places you in danger of credit refusal, or may result in a higher interest rate.

✳ Tip

When you tally your total monthly debts, use the minimum payment on your statements.

⚠ Warning

Unreported earned income cannot be used in the calculation.

192

Establish Credit

Credit isn't established overnight. Prepare yourself for financial emergencies by securing a good credit rating.

◉ Steps

1 Get cheque and savings accounts in your own name.

2 Apply for a credit card or charge card in your own name from a retail store or financial institution. Make at least a minimum payment monthly to establish a record of managing debt.

3   Apply for a loan in your name to buy jewellery, furniture or another item that will be paid off in instalments for at least a year. Make all payments on time.

4   Secure a small loan from a finance company or bank and make sure that you pay installments on time.

5   Check your credit rating by calling your creditors or ordering a copy of your credit report.

6   If you experience trouble getting a loan, ask a friend or family member to guarantee it.

Tips

Although not a credit indicator, a current or savings account shows how you manage money. Avoid bouncing cheques and add to your savings monthly.

The death of a spouse or a divorce could leave you without credit. Always establish credit in your own name.

Secure a job for several months before applying for credit.

193

Obtain a Copy of Your Credit Report

Getting a copy of your credit report is fairly simple and allows you to keep track of your credit history and check for errors.

⊚**Steps**

I   Credit ratings for millions of individuals in the UK are held by two main agencies: Equifax (equifax.co.uk) and Experian (experian.co.uk). The information they hold comprises your credit history, and will include details of unpaid bills, county court judgements (CCJs) and any previous applications for credit you have made. You can order credit reports from both companies for a cost of £2.

2   Decide whether you want to order a report online, by phone or by mail.

3   Have a credit or debit card handy if ordering online or by phone.

4   Include your personal details as requested by the agency. Sign your request and include your payment. You should receive a copy of your credit report within 15 business days.

5   Review the report closely for errors. If you do find errors, inform the agency in writing that you believe the information is in error. Include copies of any documentation to support your position.

6   Note that these companies do not, themselves, make decisions about your credit rating – they merely hold information that finance companies may use to vet credit applications.

7   Consider using one of the services that reports information from all of the major agencies – they can sometimes report information differently.

✱ Tip

One reason why some people are turned down is that they are not on the electoral roll, which exists as proof of address. If you are not registered, you should arrange to do this as soon as you can so that the details show up on your file.

194

Repair a Bad Credit History

No matter how bad your credit may be, you can take steps to make it better.

⊙ Steps

1   Always pay all of your bills on time. Late payments – payments that are 30 days late or more – may have a negative effect on your credit rating.

2   Reduce the number of credit cards you carry. Write to your creditors to request that they close your accounts and report this status change to all three credit-reporting agencies.

3   Be aware that credit failures and County Court Judgements remain on the files of credit checking agencies for six years.

4   Ask a family member or friend to guarantee a small loan or credit card to help you re-establish credit. Make your payments on time.

5 Get a yearly copy of your credit report to catch any errors (see 193 "Obtain a Copy of Your Credit Report"). If you feel there are specific circumstances which might affect your ability to obtain credit – like the loss of your job through illness or redundancy – then you can ask for a Notice of Correction to be put on your credit file. Some lenders may take this into account.

⚠ Warning

Beware of credit repair agencies that claim to be able to have County Court Judgements (CCJs) removed from your credit file: CCJ's can only be removed under specific circumstances – and when this *can* take place, the procedures are quite simple and require no outside agency to be involved.

195

Prevent Identity Theft

Some simple precautions, as well as the ability to spot trouble when it starts, may help you keep someone else from cashing in on your identity.

◎ Steps

1 Be extremely protective of your PIN numbers, especially at cashpoint machines. Try to memorise your PIN numbers, but if you have to write them down, don't leave the note in your wallet or purse.

2 Change passwords often.

3 If you live in an apartment or shared house, remove letters from your mailbox promptly. If you suddenly stop receiving mail, call the post office immediately – criminals can forge signatures to have your mail forwarded elsewhere, then obtain information that will allow them to apply for credit in your name.

4 Refuse to give your credit card number or other personal information to an unsolicited caller.

5 Tear up or shred credit card receipts, unused loan applications and any other items with personal information before throwing them away. Thieves often go through rubbish.

Cash and Credit

6   Obtain a copy of your credit report regularly to check for fraudulent accounts and other information. Report all errors.

7   Report stolen credit cards immediately.

8   Take the time to carefully review all of your bank and credit or cash card statements. Report any inconsistencies at once.

✷ Tips

If you find out that a forwarding order has been placed on your mail without your knowledge, go to the post office to check the signature and cancel the order.

To put a fraud alert on your credit file, contact the credit checking agencies Equifax or Experian.

⚠ Warning

If a relative dies, do not throw out unused cheques or other personal documents – thieves have been known to steal the identities of dead people and clean out their bank accounts.

196
Use eHow

eHow.com is the website where you can find out how to do just about everything – and purchase the products and services you need to do it. Here's how to get the most from our site.

⊙ Steps

1   Go online, type "ehow.com" in your browser's web-address field and press Enter or Return. Welcome to our home page!

2   Search for a how-to (what we call an "eHow") by typing a question – such as "How do I water a lawn?" – in the search field at the top of the page. Click "Do it" to search our database of eHows.

3   Or browse through our eHow centres, such as Home & Garden. You'll find these listed on our home page, and you can also find them via colour-coded navigation tabs that are visible on every page.

4   Read the eHow on the topic you've chosen. Note that some eHows also include video instructions.

5   As you're reading, check out tips contributed by other eHow users. (See "Ask Someone on a Date" or "Boil an Egg" for hundreds of enlightening examples.) If it's something you know how to do well, why not contribute your own tip?

6   Look for the handy shopping list that accompanies each eHow, and notice the featured books and tools. Just click on whatever you need to buy in order to get things done – or visit the eHow shop. The products you choose to buy travel with you in a virtual shopping cart as you go through the site.

7   Probe further into the eHow universe by clicking on Related eHows. Or explore other websites associated with your topic by clicking on one or more Related Sites.

8   Share favourite eHows with friends and family using our E-mail to a Friend feature. You can send any eHow – with a special message of your own – to anyone you want.

9   While you're online, sign up for our award-winning newsletter and be kept up to date on the latest eHow happenings.

10 Personalise your view of the eHow site by creating a My eHow page, for your favourite eHows, important reminders and any other goodies you choose to put there.

11 Put information in the palm of your hand by downloading any eHow to your personal device – for instant reference wherever you need it.

12 Take advantage of the time you've freed up by using our site to do the things you love. Or try something new and different: Start a business, paddle a canoe, win a sandcastle competition, plan a salsa party, redecorate your living room – or any of thousands of other things – using eHow's step-by-step instructions.

✴ Tips

If you don't have the time or desire to do a task, we can still assist you in getting the job done. Look for the Who Can Help You With This section to find people and services that can help you complete just about any task.

Check out our site regularly for new and timely features. For example, our seasonal centres come to life at Christmas time to help you enjoy the festivities in new and creative ways. And the eHow shop will help make Christmas shopping a breeze.

⚠ Warning

eHow can be highly addictive. People come to our site to find out how to do one task and end up learning a lot of other things along the way. Visit eHow.com only if you're prepared to learn more – and do more – than you ever thought you could.

Index

Index